D0630707

KNOWLEDGE SHARING IN PRACTICE

Information Science and Knowledge Management

Volume 4

Editor-in-Chief:

J. Mackenzie Owen, *University of Amsterdam, Amsterdam*

Editorial Board:

E. de Smet, *Universiteit Antwerpen, Wilrijk*
Y. Fujiwara, *Kanagawa University, Hiratsuka*
M. Hedstrom, *University of Michigan, Ann Arbor, MI*
A. Klugkist, *UB Groningen, Groningen*
K.-D. Lehmann, *Stiftung Preussischer Kulturbesitz, Berlin*
C. Lupovici, *Université de Marne la Vallee, Marne la Vallee*
A.M. Paci, *Istituto di Studi Sulla Ricerca e Documentazione Scientifica, Roma*
M. Papazoglou, *Katholieke Universiteit Brabant, Tilburg*
D.J. Waters, *The Andrew W. Mellon Foundation, New York*

KNOWLEDGE SHARING
IN PRACTICE

by

MARLEEN HUYSMAN

Department of Information Systems, Marketing and Logistics,
Faculty of Economics and Business Administration,
Vrije Universiteit Amsterdam,
Amsterdam, The Netherlands

and

DIRK DE WIT

O&I Management Partners,
Utrecht, The Netherlands

KLUWER ACADEMIC PUBLISHERS
DORDRECHT / BOSTON / LONDON

A C.I.P. Catalogue record for this book is available from the Library of Congress.

ISBN 1-4020-0584-9

Published by Kluwer Academic Publishers,
P.O. Box 17, 3300 AA Dordrecht, The Netherlands.

Sold and distributed in North, Central and South America
by Kluwer Academic Publishers,
101 Philip Drive, Norwell, MA 02061, U.S.A.

In all other countries, sold and distributed
by Kluwer Academic Publishers,
P.O. Box 322, 3300 AH Dordrecht, The Netherlands.

Printed on acid-free paper

This is a completely revised and updated translation of the original Dutch work *Kennis delen in de praktijk: Vergaren, uitwisselen en ontwikkelen van kennis met ICT*, Van Gorcum /
Stichting Management Studies (SMS), Assen, 2000.

All Rights Reserved
© 2002 Kluwer Academic Publishers
No part of the material protected by this copyright notice may be reproduced or
utilized in any form or by any means, electronic or mechanical,
including photocopying, recording, or by any information storage and
retrieval system, without written permission from the copyright owner.

Printed in the Netherlands

TABLE OF CONTENTS

PREFACE

This book is about how people working within organizations share knowledge in order to learn from and with each other. In the book, we will introduce an organizational learning model to help analyse knowledge sharing. Based on this model we will analyse how various organizations have tried to structure knowledge sharing, how ICT is used to support knowledge sharing, and the problems that organizations encountered while they were engaged in the process of structuring and supporting knowledge sharing. There are some general traps into which organizations tend to fall when they adopt a formal approach towards managing knowledge sharing. We will address these risks in more detail by discussing their origins, the effect they have and possible ways to avoid them. By emphasizing the need for knowledge sharing to become a routine for communities of practice and for investing in social capital, the book contributes to what can be called the 'second stage in the development of knowledge management'. As such, we hope that this book will succeed in providing both scholars and practitioners with a keener understanding of what is feasible and what is not when managing knowledge sharing.

The book was originally published in Dutch (see Huysman and de Wit 2000). The Dutch version of the book was written with a community of practitioners (human resources, ICT and general management) in mind. However, the present English version is geared more towards the conceptual and analytical interests of faculty and undergraduate and graduate students following courses such as knowledge management, organizational behavior, management studies, information systems, and human resource management (HRM). In addition to the academic world, the book is also useful for consultants and managers as it provides empirical insights into how to support and structure knowledge sharing.

The mixture of both an academic as well as a practical audience reflects the background of the two authors. At the time of research, Marleen Huysman was Assistant Professor at the Work and Organizational Psychology unit at the University of Delft. She is currently Associate Professor of 'Knowledge Management' at the Information Systems, Marketing and Logistics section of the Department of Economics and Business Administration, Vrije Universiteit Amsterdam. Dirk de Wit is Senior Consultant at O & I management partners in Utrecht. Formerly he worked as a researcher at the Telematica Instituut in the field of management of technology and knowledge management.

The empirical research that constitutes an important element of the book was commissioned by the Stichting (Foundation for) Management Studies (SMS) and

was supported by a committee of senior experts in the field of Human Resources as well as ICT. The following people served on the committee:
- C.W. van der Waaij, Personnel and Finance Director, Unilever (Chairman)
- J. Diekmeijer, former Director of Human Resources, IBM Netherlands
- J.W. Koole, Research, Education and Labour Market, AWVN
- F. Mulder, Professor of Information Sciences, formerly TSM Business School
- M.C. Vader, Director of Facility Services, Netherlands Railways
- J.A.L. van Rijn, business unit manager, Cap Gemini Netherlands
- C.A.M. van Zijl, Manager/Business Consultant, KPN Telecommerce
- B. van Dijkum-de Jong, Secretary, SMS

Erik Andriessen, Professor of Work and Organizational Psychology at the University of Delft and Rene Bakker, Senior Research Manager, Telematica Instituut, supervised the empirical research. The Work and Organizational Psychology section of the University of Delft also provided additional financial support.

Unfortunately, there is not enough space to thank all the individuals who helped us with the realization of the book. However, for some of them an exception must be made. We therefore wish to thank: Erik Andriessen for his advice and support for both the Dutch and English versions of this book; Barbara van Dijkum-de Jong for initiating the research and managing the committee; the Stichting Management Studies (SMS) for supporting the research; Theresa Stanton for her English translation and Robbert van Berckelaer from Kluwer Academic Publishers for his help in promoting the book. Finally, we would like to thank all those who were willing to tell us about their experiences with knowledge sharing in practice. We especially appreciate their openness and willingness to share knowledge not only about the success stories but also about the failures and what might have caused them.

Marleen Huysman
Vrije Universiteit Amsterdam

Dirk de Wit
O& I Management Partners, Utrecht
December, 2001

CHAPTER 1

INTRODUCTION

1. INTRODUCTION

The organization of today increasingly recognizes the need to support, in one way or another, knowledge-sharing among its members. Employees and specifically managers are searching, testing and using various proactive interventions to facilitate knowledge-sharing.

Knowledge-sharing is supported with different goals in mind: to acquire knowledge, to reuse knowledge, and to develop new knowledge[1]. The state-of-the-art of today's information and communication technology (ICT) makes it possible - at least in theory - to support these different purposes of knowledge-sharing.

It is, of course, still debatable whether knowledge-sharing in a specific situation will bring real benefits. Success depends on a myriad of factors, such as the added advantage for an individual to share knowledge with others, collective involvement within the organization and the correct application of ICT. Ultimately, the most important success factor for knowledge-sharing is the degree to which it is bound up in the day-to-day operations of an organization. When knowledge-sharing processes become institutionalized it suggests that all those involved in the organization consider knowledge-sharing to be a crucial part of their daily work. At that point, knowledge-sharing becomes routine instead of just another task.

We brush up against an apparent contradiction in terms here. In order to become routine practice, knowledge-sharing first requires a significant amount of organizational attention. In other words, explicit attention is necessary to obtain implicit attention. This paradoxical situation leads to a number of management dilemmas that are discussed in this book.

The practice of knowledge-sharing, on which this book is based, reveals how ten large companies are grappling with these dilemmas. In order to shed some light on these difficulties, we have analysed different knowledge-sharing practices with the help of six basic questions: *Why is knowledge shared? When is knowledge shared?*

Who shares knowledge? Where is knowledge shared? What sort of knowledge is shared? and, *How is knowledge shared?* The answers to these questions can be broken down into three critical aspects of knowledge-sharing: managing knowledge-sharing, learning from knowledge-sharing, and ICT support for knowledge-sharing. Whether or not knowledge-sharing actually becomes institutionalized and ends up becoming part of the daily routine, depends to a large extent on how much attention is given to these three integrated aspects of knowledge-sharing. Experience shows us that if we ignore these critical aspects, or handle them incorrectly, then this can easily result in knowledge-sharing being obstructed rather than promoted as routine. These three critical aspects of knowledge-sharing might create three related traps: the management trap; the individual learning trap; and, the ICT trap.

The management trap relates to the tendency to approach the need for supporting knowledge-sharing with too much empathy for the management perspective. This is one of the major pitfalls when knowledge management is introduced. When knowledge-sharing is implemented based primarily upon management's needs and not looked at from the employee's perspective, then knowledge-sharing initiatives are doomed to have a short life-span.

The individual learning trap refers to the danger of treating knowledge-sharing as a learning process for the individual while disregarding its contribution to the organization as a whole. One can only talk about *organizational learning* when there is a collective acceptance and collective use of the results of knowledge-sharing between individuals. Organizations have great difficulties structuring knowledge-sharing processes in a way that they can contribute to the improvement of the organization.

The third aspect that requires explicit attention if knowledge-sharing is to become routine is the role of ICT. There is an inherent risk involved in ICT's contribution to knowledge-sharing. This so-called ICT-trap revolves around placing too much faith in ICT's ability to improve knowledge-sharing. In practice, its role in supporting knowledge-sharing is quite limited and the 'social networks' are often more important than the electronic ones.

2. MANAGEMENT OF KNOWLEDGE-SHARING

The management of knowledge-sharing is, in our view, the structured support and guidance of (conditions for) acquiring knowledge, exchanging knowledge and using knowledge to support business processes within an organization. Strategically, knowledge-sharing involves giving systematic thought to the long term implications of knowledge in realizing the organization's objectives. Managing knowledge-sharing also has an operational short term goal which is to effectively incorporate the existing knowledge in the main production process. Only when managing knowledge-sharing contributes to organizational objectives, can it be considered successful. We focus particularly on improving organizational learning processes as a way to embed knowledge-sharing. Managing knowledge-sharing is, in our view, a way of supporting these learning processes so that it can contribute to the realization of organizational goals.

3. THIS BOOK'S CONTRIBUTION

The need to support knowledge processes in organizations has always existed. However, its importance has certainly increased in the last few years. This interest in knowledge management did not just materialize out of thin air and has a lot to do with the increasing relevance of the knowledge factor within organizations. Many books about management have focussed on this (e.g. Davenport and Prusak 1998, Drucker 1993, Nonaka and Takeuchi 1995, Porter 1990, Stewart 1997). The importance of the knowledge factor inevitably prompts one to ask how this production factor can be managed and controlled. This requirement is met through knowledge management, one of the most popular management concepts of the last decade. This book too contributes to the understanding of knowledge management. We discuss different knowledge-sharing practices, supported by ICT, that we encountered in ten large companies. Based on these experiences, we analyse the potential factors for success and failure for organizations that wish to support knowledge-sharing.

Our view of knowledge management deviates from the existing body of knowledge in various ways, and hopefully also adds an extra dimension, as a result of:

- an integrated approach

- a relational approach

- a practice-oriented approach

- a subdued approach towards ICT

- use of terminology

Merging different schools of thought: an integrated approach.
There are different schools of thought within the knowledge management sector. For example, one school of thought considers knowledge management to be a task that falls into the specific province of the ICT manager, while others argue that knowledge management is primarily a Human Resource Management (HRM) issue. There is also another group that adheres to the concept of 'Intellectual capital', which focuses in particular upon the strategic value of knowledge. Regrettably, these schools of thought have up till now learned very little from each other. This book is an attempt to bring the three groups closer to each other by selecting a more integrated approach.

Supporting interactions: a relational approach
Much of the attention given to knowledge management focuses on knowledge possessed by the individual. This book deviates from this approach in that it deals with managing knowledge-sharing *between* individuals rather than managing the knowledge *of* individuals. The focus is placed not on the individual *per se*, but on individuals as they relate to one another within the organization. This relational approach towards knowledge places greater emphasis on the level of the group, the community, the network and the organization, than on the individual employee. A relational perspective also needs structures to link up the knowledge scattered among individuals within the organization more effectively.

Based on real experiences: a practice-oriented approach
Many of our ideas about knowledge management stem from practical experiences. We selected ten different companies and analysed how knowledge-sharing takes place in practice and what their factors for success and failure were. The literature on knowledge management is renowned for featuring conceptual images in particular, which are then obliquely presented using examples from real life. These publications are full of ideas and they inspire both managers and academics alike. One drawback is that many of these images are based on experiences gained only at the preliminary stage of development or concern a project with a limited life-span. It is still unclear whether these conceptual ideas will continue to evolve successfully once they become an integral part of the day-to-day procedure.

The success of knowledge-sharing should prove itself in practice. We therefore discuss only those knowledge-sharing situations in practice through which organizations have already gained substantial long-term experience. The huge advantage to this approach is that we are able to speak more confidently about the factors for failure and success with regard to providing structures for knowledge-sharing.

ICT's supporting role: a subdued approach
Many knowledge management initiatives focus on technical systems such as knowledge and expert systems. With the boom in intranets and the introduction of Lotus Notes, many people anticipate a future in which knowledge-sharing is supported by ICT. Despite the fact that the rising star of ICT has lost something of its allure in the last few years, many people still have high expectations concerning its role in knowledge management.

In this book we do not regard technology as the panacea. In our selection of case studies the way in which knowledge was shared prevailed; how ICT enabled this knowledge-sharing was an offshoot. We distinguished three basic purposes of knowledge-sharing that offer support to different learning processes. For each basic type we subsequently analyse what ICT does, or could, contribute. We do not take it for granted that knowledge-sharing automatically becomes more effective and efficient with ICT. In fact, in this book we will describe various instances in which people when sharing knowledge, circumvent the existing ICT applications that were originally designed to support the exchange of knowledge.

'Managing Knowledge-sharing', a cautious use of terminology
We use the term 'knowledge management' with some reticence due to the ill-chosen combination of the words 'knowledge' and 'management'. Strictly speaking, managing knowledge is practically an impossible and uncalled-for task. Knowledge is, by definition, bound up with people and in this sense it not only points to human resource management but to managing everything that relates to people as well, and that does include just about everything. The concept of knowledge management as being 'people management' is then in danger of falling prey to gross generalization. Moreover, the term also elicits negative emotions, especially from employees in practice. Knowledge is often thought of as being something that resides in people's heads. Consequently, 'knowledge management' not only instinctively refers to 'people management', but also to 'brain management'.

Ultimately, the concept 'knowledge management' suggests a paradox. When compared with traditional production factors, the knowledge factor within organizations is so complex, scattered and hidden that it is considered crucial to manage it. Indeed, it is because of these very characteristics of knowledge that channelling and supporting it is an almost impossible task. The question is then whether guidance and control as core ingredients of management are indeed the right methods to achieve knowledge-sharing. It is for these reasons that we prefer using the term 'knowledge-sharing' instead of 'knowledge management'.

4. WHICH COMPANIES ARE INVOLVED?

In order to give as broad a picture as possible of the way in which organizations support their knowledge-sharing activities, we used a number of criteria when selecting cases. One important criterion was to include cases from various industry and business sectors. Many of the publications on managing knowledge focus on sectors where knowledge is the most important product, such as consultancy firms and financial corporations. Alongside business services, we also discuss knowledge processes within industry, trade and government.

A second criterion was the contribution of ICT. Given that we expected the role of ICT to differ depending on the nature of knowledge-sharing, we looked for different types of technological support, such as knowledge bases, intranets, 'electronic communities' and mind-mapping.

The decisive factor was that we would present and analyse only the genuine experiences of companies. This selection principle precluded studying a large number of potentially interesting, hypothetical case studies. Upon closer examination, it proved that the different organizations had hardly gained any experience in managing knowledge-sharing, despite the often very interesting initiatives. Of course, a prior condition was that organizations should be willing to contribute towards the realization of this book. Although some doors remained closed on a couple of occasions, most organizations did not balk at providing us with information.

We finally ended up with a selection of ten situations in which knowledge-sharing in the organization was supported by management. Table 1 gives an overview of this. In this table the cases have been divided up according to the medium used to share knowledge, how far the knowledge-sharing practices have evolved, and whether the organization expressly considers the knowledge-sharing practice to be knowledge management. Companies that have introduced knowledge-sharing, as a rule, have less experience than companies that have already implemented knowledge-sharing.

Table 1. Overview of different case studies

Organizations	Medium	Stage of implementation of knowledge-sharing	Use of the 'knowledge management' concept
Cap Gemini	Personal networks Intranet	Networks: institutionalized Intranet implemented	Personal networks: no Intranet: yes
IBM	Intranet	Implemented	Yes
ING Barings	Intranet	Introduced	No
Ministry of Housing	Digital Platforms	Institutionalized	No
NN	Personal networks Knowledge system	Institutionalized	Yes (following institutionalization)
Railways	Mobile knowledge base	Institutionalized	No
Postbank	Knowledge base	Institutionalized	No
Schiphol	Reports and intranet	Implemented	Yes
Stork	Reports	Institutionalized	No
Unilever	Knowledge base Mind-mapping	Implemented	Yes

The research is based on an analysis of conversations and written documentation with more than fifty people who are actively using knowledge management in practice. The objective was, with each situation, to approach both managers and those taking the initiative, as well as the people who actually share their knowledge. The final case descriptions that emerged from this were subsequently shown once again to both the interviewees as well as the contact person within the organization for approval. Based on this we are confident that the descriptions in this book reflect the impressions of those involved.

The selection of ten case studies means that the study is not representative of the way in which knowledge management is supported in organizations in general. But being representative was not our intention. The main objective behind describing and analysing the practice was to provide insights into the way in which a number of experienced companies handle knowledge-sharing. They are companies with years of experience in structuring knowledge-sharing, and they all do this in different ways. Through this we can reflect on the factors for success and failure from the different case studies.

5. WHERE ARE THE LIMITATIONS?

This book mainly focuses upon structured forms of knowledge-sharing within large companies. By using this particular approach insights into the following are not taken into account:

— unstructured types of knowledge-sharing,

— knowledge-sharing between companies,

— knowledge-sharing within Small and Medium-sized Enterprises (SME)

The knowledge-sharing practices that we discuss in this book are all, to a lesser or greater extent, structured practices. Members of the organization purposefully intervene in order to facilitate knowledge-sharing. With this considered approach towards the practice of knowledge-sharing, we do not shed light on the question of how unstructured forms of knowledge-sharing can be supported and the role of ICT in this area. Due to this approach issues such as managing 'implicit' knowledge and 'situated knowledge' are seldom raised at first. However, it will appear that the unstructured types of knowledge-sharing are often representative of actual day-to-day practice while the structured forms are more likely to ascribe to the 'espoused theories' (Argyris and Schön 1978).

Another important limitation of this book is the amount of attention we give to knowledge-sharing *within* organizations. Interorganizational knowledge-sharing processes receive practically no attention whatsoever. This does not mean that knowledge-sharing between organizations is a less important issue. In fact, one might even argue that nowadays the opposite is true. With the increasing tendency towards competition, globalization, and interorganizational cooperation, the need for insights into when and how organizations exchange knowledge with one another is increasing. This issue requires a separate study and is only presented in passing in this book.

Another important restriction is that the book only deals with knowledge-sharing in large companies. Small and Medium-sized Enterprises (SMEs) are therefore under-represented. According to Beijerse (1998), SMEs have several specific characteristics that could make different demands upon structured knowledge-sharing:

–   SMEs deal with a relatively smaller profit margin which means that there is less financial elbow room for knowledge management projects.

–   SMEs are relatively speaking less preoccupied with long-term developments. This can hamper initiatives for structured knowledge-sharing.

–   The limited number of staff employed at an SME reduces the opportunity for initiatives. At smaller enterprises it is not so necessary to structure knowledge-sharing because staff encounter one another much more quickly in an unstructured fashion.

6. WHAT DOES THE BOOK LOOK LIKE?

The first part presents the theoretical background that helps enhance one's understanding of the importance of knowledge sharing as well as providing ways to analyse it. Chapter two discusses theoretical ideas about the growing importance of managing knowledge in organizations. It starts with a discussion about the knowledge factor in relation to society and the current situation in which organizations find themselves. In this way, we place knowledge management in its historical context and explain why it might be more than just a management fad. We go on to discuss a number of views on knowledge management. 'Organizational learning' is subsequently introduced as a theoretical framework that enables different viewpoints to be integrated. Chapter three discusses the theoretical background of the notion of 'organizational learning' and how it will help in analysing knowledge-sharing in organizations. A model for organizational learning serves as a guide to help further examine three different knowledge-sharing processes discussed in part two of this book. These three processes of knowledge-sharing include:

–   *Acquiring knowledge:* knowledge-sharing with the organization as knowledge provider.

–   *Reusing knowledge:* knowledge-sharing with the individual as knowledge provider.

–   *Developing knowledge:* knowledge-sharing with the community as knowledge provider.

In part two of this book: "Practices of knowledge-sharing", three separate chapters present different experiences from practice which have been split up into the three purposes of knowledge-sharing listed above. Chapter four presents knowledge-sharing practices that involve acquiring knowledge from individuals. Knowledge-sharing practices at the Postbank, NN and Netherlands Railways are presented here. Chapter five highlights knowledge-sharing in the form of knowledge reuse between individuals. The companies that were examined include ING Barings, Cap Gemini, IBM and Amsterdam Airport Schiphol. In Chapter six we highlight the practices of knowledge-sharing for the purpose of knowledge sharing within communities. Stork, the Ministry of Housing and Unilever provide examples of this.

Part three of this book: "Critical Analysis", gives an analysis of knowledge-sharing in practice as it is described in the preceding sections. This was carried out by asking the following questions: Why is knowledge shared? When is knowledge shared? Who shares knowledge? Where is knowledge shared? What type of knowledge is shared? and, How is knowledge shared? Answers to these questions lead to the identification of three general traps or risks which organizations might run into once they became involved in supporting knowledge-sharing. These three traps touch upon the three most important aspects of knowledge-sharing: managing knowledge-sharing, the contribution to organizational learning, and ICT's role in this. Chapter seven discusses the 'management trap'. This points to the dangers of anticipating management's needs above all else during knowledge-sharing at the expense of the needs of the individual. Chapter eight discusses the so-called 'individual learning trap'. This trap indicates the danger of paying particular attention to knowledge-sharing for the benefit of individual learning at the expense of the collective. Finally, Chapter nine deals with the 'ICT trap'. Here we target the dominant role that ICT plays in supporting knowledge-sharing, which in itself contains inherent risks. Each chapter deals with the background of the trap in question, and different measures that can be taken to avoid the trap are also discussed.

The book concludes with Chapter 10 "Epilogue" which maps out the future direction that knowledge management might take. The next generation of the knowledge management concept will focus more attention on institutionalizing knowledge-sharing. Indeed the term 'social capital' is looked at in this chapter as a potentially fruitful way of approaching the complexity of managing knowledge-sharing as discussed earlier. This final chapter ends with a number of recommendations to both support and encourage knowledge-sharing from this perspective.

PART 1

THEORETICAL BACKGROUND

In the following two chapters a theoretical background is given which helps the reader understand the importance of both knowledge-sharing and the different ways of analysing it. Chapter two discusses theoretical ideas about the growing importance of managing knowledge in organizations. It starts with a discussion about the knowledge factor in relation to society and the current situation in which organizations find themselves. We discuss a number of views on knowledge management. 'Organizational learning' is subsequently introduced as a theoretical framework that enables different viewpoints to be integrated.

Chapter three discusses the theoretical background of the notion of 'organizational learning' and how it will help in analysing knowledge-sharing in organizations. A model for organizational learning serves as a guide to help further examine the three different knowledge-sharing processes that are discussed in part two of this book. These three processes of knowledge-sharing include:

- *Acquiring knowledge:* knowledge-sharing with the organization as knowledge owner.

- *Reusing knowledge:* knowledge-sharing with the individual as knowledge owner.

- *Developing knowledge:* knowledge-sharing with the community as knowledge owner.

CHAPTER 2

THEORIES ON MANAGING KNOWLEDGE

1. INTRODUCTION

Managers have a seemingly endless desire for new concepts (Abrahamson 1996). One such concept that has attracted a lot of attention in recent years and continues to be in the limelight is knowledge management. It is almost as if the meaning of knowledge has been rediscovered. Yet as fresh as the hype might be, this concept too is already showing the first signs of flagging. It seems that a management trend only lasts as long as it takes for a new manager to shine. The golden age of knowledge management has come and gone, 'communities of practice', portals and e-learning are the latest buzz-words.

At the same time, more books and articles are being published on the practice of knowledge management. A number of these publications have revealed just how difficult it is for an organization to introduce knowledge management within their company (e.g Davenport and Prusak 1998, Weggeman 2000). A knowledge management research report (KPMG 2000) also indicates that while it might be true that knowledge management has finally been placed on the management agenda, nevertheless managers still find it hard to allow knowledge-sharing to successfully run its course. An important reason why knowledge management fails is because the focus on technology is often too intimidating, a fact which is often not fully appreciated by managers.

As soon as a knowledge management project fails managers tend to throw the baby out with the bathwater and focus on a completely new trend. Meanwhile, managers are still wrestling with the same old questions:

- What do we know as a company and how do we exploit this knowledge?

- How can we use the knowledge of employees to strengthen core competences?

- How does a company set about mobilizing the brainpower of its employees?

- What happens to the knowledge and the social networks when an employee leaves for another job?

- What happens to empirical knowledge if people leave the company prematurely?

- How can an organization ensure that people are prepared to share their knowledge and make their expertise available to the organization?

- How does an organization deal with the changing nature of products and services, the vanishing boundaries between departments, and the increasing importance of the group's result as opposed to individual performance?

Managers, consultants and researchers have come up with both practical solutions and conceptual answers for questions such as those listed above. Some companies opt for technical solutions while others tend to stretch their training budgets to the limit. Some businesses start reorganization programmes hoping that knowledge management can play a leading role there too. When faced with this tangled mass of different viewpoints, it is often unclear to organizations just what knowledge management could mean to them or whether they should allow themselves to sidestep the issue altogether. In this chapter we explain why it is important to focus on the knowledge flows within a company. We highlight various ideas about knowledge management and present our own views on how knowledge-sharing is managed.

2. BACKGROUND

It is more than thirty years ago that our language first became enriched with terms such as knowledge work and knowledge worker. Drucker introduced these terms in the 1960s to highlight a key change that was taking place in society. Knowledge had by this time become a key component in people's work as well as an important characteristic of the post-capitalist society. The post-capitalist society is characterised by innovation, creativity, new discoveries and inventiveness; terms that were no less important thirty years ago than they are today. These are impressive words to show that important changes were taking place in the way in which organizations functioned and the role that people played within society.

A wealth of similar impressive terms have come and gone over the years (Abrahamson 1996; Kieser 1997). Just as the rise of the information and service-oriented society was ultra-fashionable about a decade ago, it is now clear that in today's competitive environment it is not just information for its own sake that is important. Everything revolves around what a company or an individual does with that information.

Information becomes knowledge when a human being forms justified true beliefs about the world (Choo et al, 2000). In organizations, this justification of knowledge becomes a public process that can be very fragile and political (Von Krogh 1998). How this process of what we call 'organizational learning' takes shape and how it shapes knowledge will be discussed in the second part of this chapter. First, we will discuss the importance of knowledge in organizations. In at least three highly interrelated areas, changes have taken place that have spurred on the present interest in knowledge, the knowledge economy and the knowledge society, and vice versa. Although these areas are interdependent, we will briefly discuss each one of them separately below under the headings: changes in work, technology and ways of doing business.

Changes in work
When changes take place in society it is natural that this should also precipitate a change in skills among individuals as well as a shift in the kind of knowledge that people need and the way in which they acquire that knowledge. In the classic tripartite of production factors; capital, land and labour, labour refers to human abilities such as strength, skills, knowledge, and inventiveness. While some would say that it is still too early to dub knowledge a new production factor, it has certainly gained in importance alongside the traditional production factors. People bring their talents with them, and increasingly this is in the form of knowledge rather than brute strength. In this respect, the knowledge that people have acquired ought to be valued. Working with your head on a variety of abstract levels is the most commonplace method of working in the knowledge economy.

If there is a clear dividing line between the information society and the knowledge economy then perhaps this can be found on the level of people's skills and the value of the training they have followed. In the information society education guaranteed a career, in the knowledge economy education is just the admission ticket. The speed with which the knowledge worker renews codified knowledge and can forget old knowledge determines his or her career development. In the knowledge society the emphasis is on social relationships and human interaction as a work trait (e.g. Botkin 1999, Cohen and Prusak 2000, Hansen et al, 1999). Empathy, judgement, creativity, and relationship-building are characteristics that distinguish the knowledge worker from the office employee (Nahapiet and Ghosal 1998). In such a knowledge-based company, there are no subordinates, only associates. In practice, this means, among other things, that individuals are responsible for their own position within the company. Knowledge workers have to continuously ask themselves how they contribute to both their own as well as the organization's mission and objectives.

Knowledge worker
In many companies creating or recycling knowledge is very important for continuity, but we should not allow ourselves to become too bogged down with knowledge work. A lot of administrative work is not automatically knowledge work

just because we now happen to find ourselves in a knowledge economy. Similarly, every production employee is not necessarily a knowledge worker, although they will certainly possess knowledge about a product, process or service, which could be beneficial to the company. A knowledge worker works primarily in the fields of R&D, advertising, training and the professional service sector (legal representatives, accountants and consultants). Singling out this group of professional workers already hints at an ideological undertone: they represent the elite within the white collar proletariat. Service-oriented work can be found in public and private organizations and consists, for example, of administrative work, customer services, and processing claims at insurance companies.

Changes in work also demand a 'different way of managing'. Hanssen and Von Oettinger (2001) argue the need for T-shaped managers. Managers can fulfil the role that has been dreamed up for knowledge brokers and can function as human portals. The T-shaped manager earnestly looks beyond the horizon of his or her own business unit and tries to build bridges between the different types of expertise within the organization. A kind of organizational net is stretched over the existing structures enabling managers to learn from one another.

A new role: the knowledge broker

The role of knowledge broker in supporting knowledge-sharing has often been stressed (Hargadon 1998, Leonard and Swap 2000, Scarbrough and Swan 2002, Wenger 1998). Various knowledge broker roles can be identified (Wenger 1998):

- *Boundary spanners* – who take care of one specific boundary of a knowledge community
- *Roamers* – going from place to place, creating an informal web of connections
- *Outposts* – bringing back news from the front and exploring new territories.

Changes in technology

For many managers, knowledge management is synonymous with technology. It fits neatly into the data-information-knowledge equation that was mentioned earlier. The database-management systems of the 1970s were followed in the 1980s by the information management systems. The 1990s saw the launch of the 'knowledge based management system'. The parallel goes even further. The first 15 years of the 'computer revolution' consisted mainly of automating labour-intensive tasks. It was primarily all about data processing. After this, information service provision and all kinds of information systems held sway for two decades. It is currently the knowledge intensive organizations that dearly wish to have their knowledge flows supported.

3. KNOWLEDGE MANAGEMENT AND ICT

One key characteristic of our society is that it is generally believed that technological and economic developments have been influencing its growth and prosperity for centuries. This is why we associate today's society with information and communication technology, biotechnology and medical technology. In addition, specific technological innovations have had a major impact on society. Examples of these significant technologies are the clock, the windmill and the steam engine, or more recently car engineering, electrical engineering and biotechnology. Information and communication technology is an essential technology because it is drastically changing life and work in society. Information and communication technologies act as catalysts in the creation of the post-industrial or information society (Drucker 1993). We are witnessing all kinds of phenomena that point towards even more digitization. The continuous rise in the sale of personal computers (PCs) for example is an indication of how information technology has permeated the home, through which conditions for the further automation of society are created. The financial services sector has become completely dependent upon ICT. Email, mobile telephones, and Internet have become standard practice for the consumer and the business world alike. ICT is now a part of product manufacturing in practically every production process.

Many people see possibilities for ICT to contribute to these knowledge intensive organizations, given that ICT unites hitherto divided dataflows for production, marketing, logistics and accounting (Teece, 1998). Intranets strengthen information channels between strategic and operational management. Extranets, EDI or network technology accelerate communications and transactions with suppliers. The new networks will continuously change their composition. ICT makes this change possible. While ICT is for some companies a core competence to achieve a strategic advantage, the examples for knowledge-sharing are still relatively limited. For example, while the theoretical advantages of GroupWare and GDSS are fully known, in practice many companies do not go further than using databases and intranets. The development of new applications certainly offers a wealth of new opportunities, but the key issue is how people actually use them. Later on we will discuss in more detail how companies exploit ICT in their knowledge exchange activities.

Knowledge intensive enterprise

A financial services company that invests heavily in ICT is still not a knowledge intensive enterprise. Even organizations where copious amounts of data and information flows represent the core of their business cannot automatically be defined as knowledge intensive companies. When we take bank transactions for example as a model, we notice that a lot of data flows in the primary process from one account holder to another. Many banks and insurance companies have jumped onto the 'data-warehousing and data-processing' bandwagon in order to cash in on their hidden treasures. With this they hope to obtain a keener grasp of customer behaviour so that they will eventually be able to provide a more individually tailored service. There are still few successful examples of this technique being effectively applied to increase knowledge on customers. Most financial companies are also examples of information-intensive enterprises. Even though learning from clients is not an explicit objective here, the knowledge bases do fulfil a role in providing a service to the customer.

Changes in doing business

The main message in many books on knowledge management is that knowledge is an essential element of a company's ability to compete. In order to stay competitive and function innovatively, knowledge, and ultimately knowledge development, has assumed an important role. What used to be information management in the information society, has now become knowledge management in the knowledge society. Before the information society has even had a chance to get off the ground we have already started talking about a knowledge economy and a knowledge society. Digitization, 'mass customization', the network economy, and globalization influence the existence of the knowledge economy (Jacobs 1999).

These trends determine the products and services that we consume as well as how we work to produce these products and services. People have started to learn in a different way and are using other skills, products contain an increasingly higher quota of embedded knowledge, more knowledge is needed to design products and there is increased pressure from outside to deliver new products faster.

Knowledge enterprise

A knowledge enterprise is sometimes looked upon as an organization in which information use takes on a life of its own (Stewart, 1997). Hotel chains that process the information they gather on their guests so that they can standardize their customers service world-wide are on their way to becoming knowledge based enterprises. Or take Boeing who realised the design of their Boeing 777 using simulations in a 3D-design environment. The importance of such simulations is that different engineers are pulled into the design process much more quickly and therefore have to share their knowledge with each other at an earlier stage.

Companies are under pressure to bring products onto the market more quickly, and these same products also have to be of a higher quality and be better tailored to the customer's individual needs. At the same time, the shelf-life of existing products is becoming shorter. On the one hand, this is because more products are trying to score points through their projected image and instant appeal and are therefore more likely to be susceptible to the dictates of fashion. On the other hand, specific technological developments accelerate this process. This change in product life produces different types of reactions from managers, such as the desire to recycle people's knowledge, which in turn might force people to record their knowledge. At the same time companies need to stimulate people's creativity. In order to serve the market better, both qualitatively and quantitatively, many companies view knowledge as the tool with which they can achieve these new goals.

4. KNOWLEDGE MANAGEMENT

In the section above we discussed a number of changes that cause us to look upon our surroundings as an environment where, in a knowledge economy, knowledge workers can shape their knowledge intensive organization. Yet we have still barely scratched the surface regarding the subject of knowledge management. In many ways, it is an open and shut case: knowledge management is a broad concept that can be interpreted in many different ways. Some people see knowledge management as being all about controlling and channelling knowledge flows within the company, assuming that these can be codified. Software-companies, on the other hand, often see knowledge management as a way to extract 'knowledge' from complex information flows, while other people interpret knowledge management as the act of making knowledge accessible to professionals inside the company or, in some cases, actually guiding professionals within the company.

Knowledge management initiatives come from many different sources. Initiatives sometimes spring up from within a group of individuals who then follow them through within their own organization. Ideas also often emanate from high-ranking managers who have witnessed successful examples when attending a conference. However, knowledge exchange initiatives are frequently carried out in many companies with a total disregard for the strategic pros and cons. In a handful of cases strategic grounds are used at a later date to justify the initiative.

Knowledge management strategies
Broadly speaking, there are two strategies that companies can use to manage their knowledge. In the recycling model companies make a one-off, substantial investment in their knowledge (assets) and ICT. They also use young graduates to meet their clients' needs. Codifying knowledge is the key word here and so management stimulates people to use and add to the knowledge database. Relatively large teams are also assigned to each partner. The company is aiming for huge profits with comparatively small margins. This strategy is evident in companies such as Ernst and Young, Cap Gemini and Dell Computers. On the other hand, there is also the strategy of personalizing knowledge as is the case at consultancy firms such as McKinsey, Boston Consultancy or Hewlett Packard. Their economic model is based upon creating high profit margins by coming up with tailor-made solutions for individual clients. People work in small teams and the goal is specifically to create networks of people. The ICT support is geared towards facilitating these networks. People are

rewarded for sharing knowledge with their colleagues. The trouble-shooting skills of the people are greater, while partners are often heavily involved in the selection procedure (Hansen et al, 1999).

Knowledge management and sharing knowledge can be approached in many different ways. Three of the most common perspectives are given below:

− a technical perspective

− a process perspective

− an intellectual capital perspective.

So far these three approaches have consistently failed to capitalize on their respective insights. This is quite remarkable when one considers that all three contain valuable elements. We therefore advocate a more integrated approach that reaps the benefits of each one of these uniquely valuable contributions.

4.1 Knowledge management as a technique

One tradition that has definitely made its mark upon knowledge management is that of knowledge systems, representing perhaps the most technical approach towards knowledge. This technical approach deals with knowledge from a stock perspective (Weggeman,1997). The stock vision focuses on *storing knowledge* to make it more accessible. The stock approach is identified with, for example, knowledge bases, expert systems and decision support systems.

We can see the technical interpretation, for example, when expert systems are used in law firms (Gottschalk 1999). In addition, there are many intranets that are based on this approach. Although research has revealed that it is not possible to turn knowledge into an object in intelligent computer systems, there are practical applications that can be realised (Malhotra, 2000).

This point of view presupposes that knowledge can be made explicit and subjected to rules. For a specific type of problem this is a legitimate point of view. However, the stock approach is often inert and reduces the individual to a mere information source whose knowledge can be codified. This approach is rooted in a strong, rational view of the world and is typical of the early knowledge management initiatives in Western companies. The danger of the stock approach is that one can become fixated on storing information (rather than knowledge).

With the advent of more advanced ICT, the flow-approach toward knowledge can also be supported using technology. The flow vision places the emphasis on transferring knowledge through personal contacts (Weggeman, 1997). In the flow approach, knowledge is an inherent element of the work processes within an organization. The flow approach focuses on the communicative potential of ICT, such as for example GroupWare. Countless new ICT-applications bridge the distance in time and place and support processes such as knowledge exchange, knowledge dissemination and interpreting knowledge. Phenomena such as on-the-job-training, cooperation between geographically dispersed teams, call centres and help-desks can be more easily structured when they are embedded in new work methods.

4.2   Knowledge as a process

Thinking in processes offers a powerful stimulus to analyse current and future knowledge flows. In the mid-1990s, 'business process re-engineering' offered a tool to those companies, which found themselves in serious difficulties. When processes were analysed the importance of carrying out a good analysis of the information flow became apparent. It was from this angle that the BPR gurus began to look at knowledge flows in which the terms 'knowledge' and 'information' were used indiscriminately. Exponents of the process approach stress the dynamic nature of knowledge management

Knowledge is more than just *information*. In addition, it contains experiences, skills and insights. These forms of knowledge are produced during day-to-day interactions. The flow vision of knowledge as discussed above has a dominant role in the process approach of knowledge management. An individual learning perspective is closely related to the process approach as learning is geared towards individual knowledge development and increasing competences. In the knowledge society it is very important for organizations that individual employees continue to develop their knowledge. The individual is the knowledge vessel and the learning potential is linked to individual learning abilities. It is the company's job to set the organization up in such a way that it can derive the maximum benefit from individuals within the company.

One important aspect of this approach is that of skills management. There is a relationship here with the concept of competences. It concerns analysing the skills that the company needs and the skills that the people themselves possess. Team leaders and people have a role to play here too. The skills have sometimes been recorded in a database, such as for example at IBM and Akzo-Nobel. The emphasis on learning indeed highlights one of the more difficult aspects of knowledge management.

4.3   Knowledge as intellectual capital

Alongside these points of view, there is also another school of thought that perceives knowledge as being one of the key resources of an organization. Proponents of this approach concentrate on making the added value of knowledge to a company more explicit (e.g. Edvinsson and Malone 1997, Grant 1996, Stewart 1997, Teece 1998). In this regard, some strive to make knowledge explicit in financial terms. An increasingly larger group of 'knowledge management experts' indeed maintains that knowledge cannot be expressed in economic terms. In this instance, making the value of the knowledge factor explicit concerns in particular deliberately improving and supporting knowledge assets. The reasoning behind this is simple. If we look at the difference in value between the stocks and the book value of a company then a large section of the difference resides in the intellectual capital of a company. Even more significantly, knowledge intensive companies often stand out because of their low book value. Knowledge companies rent their office space, lease their cars and hire out their trucks.

A company's most important asset is its intellectual capital. Intellectual capital consists of human capital, social capital and structural capital. The organizational infrastructure that is adapted to knowledge work is the 'structural capital'. The knowledge of an employee is referred to as 'human capital'. The shared situated knowledge of communities and networks is referred to as 'social capital'. The underlying question to all of this is what happens if those who possess the intellectual capital, walk out of the office one day never to return.

Knowledge management perceived from the intellectual capital approach is primarily geared towards building up structural capital. The focus is on how the work is carried out with continuous attention for using and developing knowledge so that the organization can function effectively. Structural capital includes issues such as business processes, how the work is organized, rewards for work, training, customer relations and, in particular, the information technology that already exists in-house (such as networks and databases). Structural capital ensures that human and social capital flourishes; it supports the knowledge input and build-up of knowledge within the organization.

Measuring intellectual capital
A familiar tool for measuring intellectual capital is the Skandia Navigator. Opinions are divided regarding the usefulness of measuring knowledge. Glazer (1998) maintains that it is futile for knowledge managers to manage their 'assets' as long as no good performance criteria exist. The value of knowledge management will remain limited in the eyes of the corporate environment as long as its value cannot be expressed in figures. The main objective: making the additional value of knowledge visible is adhered to, but as long as it does not manage to gain a foothold in the accountancy world, it will

be a waste of time. Moreover, despite the Skandia Navigator, plenty of questions remain unanswered such as "Do you measure knowledge itself, or the knowledge transporter?"

5. TOWARDS AN ALTERNATIVE APPROACH TO MANAGING KNOWLEDGE

Each one of the three approaches discussed above has its own useful aspects that call for integration. Firstly, the technical approach leads to the realization that the structuring or management of knowledge can be supported by different ICT applications. However, it is important that the managers of an organization understand the different possibilities as well as the shortcomings.

Secondly, the process approach towards knowledge-sharing provides insights into knowledge management, emphasizing the knowledge development process and how knowledge is passed on between individuals. It is particularly important for the ICT professional who is busy with knowledge bases to have a good understanding of these inter-relational processes.

Finally, the intellectual capital movement sheds light on the need to treat knowledge-sharing as a strategic issue, which in turn has to contribute to the organization's goals.

Integrating these three aspects requires a general theoretical framework, which also provides the keys to structuring knowledge-sharing in practice. The 'organizational learning' concept (see Figure. 1) lends itself perfectly to this.

By focussing attention on the way in which learning takes place within organizations, we deliberately zoom in on the different knowledge-sharing processes within organizations. Organizational learning involves different types and levels of knowledge-sharing. Knowledge-sharing forms the basis for organizational learning; it is by sharing knowledge - in whatever manner - that organizations learn. To set organizational learning processes upon the right track - in other words to manage organizational learning processes so that they contribute to the organization's goals - it is of paramount importance to support existing knowledge-sharing processes and to initiate new ones. Knowledge management is nothing other than managing knowledge-sharing, or rather learning processes. It directs the attention to the importance of creating the correct learning environment in order to maintain knowledge productivity - and with it the allure of the professional as a knowledge worker - at its optimum level (Kessels 2000).

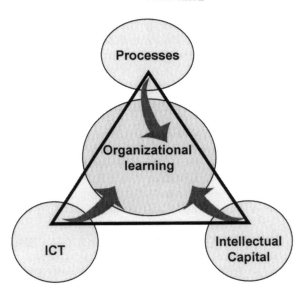

Figure 1. Relationship between different points of view and organizational learning

The concept of organizational learning also supports the idea of intellectual capital. This view maintains that it is strategically important for organizations to focus attention on the development, support and improvement of their internal knowledge housekeeping practices. The normative approach of organizational learning, namely expressed in 'the learning organization', has followed these tenets for years. Some authors even go so far as to argue that the competitive strength of an organization lies in its potential for organizational learning (e.g. De Geus 1988, Pedler e.a. 1991, Prahalad and Hamel 1993, Senge 1990).

Learning organizations
By 'Learning Organization' a specific type of organization is meant; one that has been set up in such a way (culturally as well as structurally) that continuous self-analysis and improvement can be guaranteed. Literature about the 'Learning Organization' is particularly geared towards advice and intervention and looks upon the 'Learning Organization' as an entity worth aspiring to. In turbulent environments, in which organizations sometimes find themselves, the theory is that it is only the 'Learning Organization' that will be able to keep its head above water and even gain a competitive edge. Despite its popularity, the literature on the 'Learning Organization' does have one disadvantage in that the more basic aspects of the learning processes have still not yet been addressed.

Analysing the role that ICT plays in supporting learning processes requires a less technology driven and individual cognitive approach than we are used to in the knowledge management literature. Putting it simply, the role of ICT is therefore viewed as follows. To support knowledge workers in their work we can extract (part of) the knowledge from people's heads and incorporate it in systems. In the case of learning processes the role of ICT is more of a by-product and more focussed on the collective processes of knowledge-sharing. We regard knowledge management as being a way to support organizational learning processes so that they can contribute to the realization of the organization's objectives. Organizational learning is the process of organizational knowledge (re)production.

Organizational knowledge
Organizational knowledge is the knowledge - laid down in rules, procedures, strategies, technologies, conditions, paradigms, cultures and terms of reference - that helps an organization to deal with its members. It is important that organizational knowledge is independent of the individual actor who uses this knowledge. The knowledge must be able to survive substantial staff changes within the organization.

In the next chapter we provide insights into the process of 'organizational learning' . We will discuss a number of general theoretical aspects. We will then go on to illustrate how organizations learn, that is to say how they produce and reproduce knowledge. Based on social constructivist notions of knowledge construction, we introduce an organizational learning model that is made up of three types or goals of knowledge-sharing practices: knowledge acquisition, knowledge reuse and knowledge development. The support given to these three types of knowledge-sharing will form the basis of the discussion in part two of this book.

6. SUMMARY

Knowledge is receiving more and more attention within organizations. Some authors are already talking about a knowledge economy in which knowledge represents the most important production factor. Changes in production methods, in the way in which labour is allocated, in technology and in business styles mean that managers feel the need to manage knowledge more effectively.

The 'knowledge management' concept, which emanates from this emphasis on knowledge, has been present in organizations for some time now. As with most management concepts, there is not just one unequivocal approach towards knowledge management. The concept is tackled from a technical point of view as well as from a process approach which revolves around human interactions and from a more strategic perspective whereby knowledge represents the intellectual capital of the organization.

Given that all three approaches add value to our understanding of managing knowledge-sharing, it would be useful to integrate them. The idea of 'organizational learning' offers a good framework in which to activate this integration. Chapter three will elaborate on this link between knowledge-sharing and organizational learning.

CHAPTER 3

ORGANIZATIONAL LEARNING

1. INTRODUCTION

In this book we make the link between knowledge management and organizational learning. We consider knowledge management to be a management tool that can be used to support organizational learning in such a way that it contributes to the realization of the goals of an organization. Organizations are engaged in managing learning when they are involved in processes, in whatever shape or form, that initiate or support knowledge sharing within the organization.

Linking knowledge management with organizational learning is helpful as it connects the various levels within an organization: individual, group and organizational. When knowledge management is held up as being the management of organizational learning processes, then the link with the organization as a whole and its organizational goals is made clearer. This in fact, seems to be one of the key problems organizations face when engaging in knowledge management as it is often geared towards individuals within an organization rather than towards the organization as a whole (see Chapter 7).

Organizational learning involves different types of knowledge-sharing. Knowledge-sharing provides the basis for organizational learning; it is by sharing knowledge - in whatever form this might take - that organizations learn - irrespective of the way in which this takes place and the results obtained. In order to set organizational learning processes on the right track - in other words, to manage organizational learning processes in such a way that they contribute to the organization's goals - it is of paramount importance both to support existing knowledge-sharing processes and to initiate new ones. When knowledge management is looked upon as a support for organizational learning then these specific activities are stressed. Knowledge management is therefore nothing other than the management of knowledge-sharing processes, or rather learning processes.

The remainder of this chapter is given over to a discussion on knowledge management from an organizational learning point of view. First and foremost we begin by examining several theoretical premises upon which the concept of organizational learning is based. A theoretical framework is drawn up based on the social constructivist approach. This framework will serve as an analytical model when the knowledge-sharing processes that are considered to form part of organizational learning are analysed.

2. THE THEORETICAL APPROACH OF ORGANIZATIONAL LEARNING

In this section we provide a more systematic and conceptual understanding of the process of 'organizational learning'[2] We begin by discussing a number of general theoretical issues linked to the notion of organizational learning. A description of how organizations learn is subsequently given, this is how they construct and reconstruct knowledge, and where new knowledge comes from.

Without doubt, management terms such as 'learning company' and 'the learning organization', etc. have gained good currency among academics and organizational practitioners. One plausible explanation for this interest is that learning organizations are generally seen as the solution to problems caused by hierarchical and bureaucratic organizations. With a learning organization, one generally refers to a specific type of organization that is organized – both culturally and structurally – so that innovation, flexibility, and improvement can be guaranteed. Literature on the learning organization perceives learning as being something worth striving for. Consequently, the literature predominantly focuses on providing best-practices and models in order for consultants and managers to intervene. Its argument in short is as follows: within today's turbulent environments, only learning organizations are able to survive and thus gain a competitive advantage (e.g. Garvin 1993, Marquardt 1996, Pedler 1991, Senge 1990).

Ideas on 'the learning organization' are different from ideas on the process of 'organizational learning'. The following premise on the learning of organizations is typical of the literature that treats organizational learning as a process. Organizational learning is a basic element in the evolution of organizations; every organization learns, regardless of how it operates. Whether or not this learning will result in the organization improving or renewing its organizational knowledge ('good learning') cannot be determined beforehand and therefore continues to be a subject for research.

Various authors have argued that there is a growing dichotomy between these two streams of research: the learning organization stream and the organizational learning stream (Easterby-Smith 1999, Huysman 2000a, Tsang 1997). These two streams represent two almost contrasting perspectives (see Table 2).

Despite its popularity, the ideas concerning the learning organization more often than not lack a solid theoretical, as well as empirical, foundation. This is a clear disadvantage as insights into the way organizations learn are a necessary precondition to construct prescriptive arguments on how organizations should learn. In other words, in order to create a learning organization that is good at organizational learning, we first need to have a more conceptual understanding about the processes of organizational learning. This kind of organizational learning perspective on the learning organization seems to be a fruitful combination.

Table 2. Some differences between the learning organization and organizational learning

	Organizational learning	*Learning organization*
Outcome	Potential organizational change	Organizational improvement
Motive	Organizational evolution	Competitive advantage
Writings	Descriptive	Prescriptive
Objective of writings	Theory building	Intervention
Stimulus	Emergent	Planned
Target Audience	Academic	Practice
Scientific background	Decision theory, Organization studies	Organizational development, Strategic management

In this book we will use ideas taken from the approach that sees organizational learning as a process. By discussing ways to support this process so that it contributes to organizational improvement, our general discussion and perspective on supporting knowledge-sharing supports the 'organizational learning perspective on the learning organization', as mentioned above.

Cyert and March (1963) were among the first proponents of such an approach. In their 'Behavioral theory of the firm' they argued that organizations learn by adapting their objectives, attention and search routines to their experiences. More than a decade later, March and Olsen (1976) showed that, as a result of often irrational organizational behaviour, learning is full of hindrances and shortcomings. Two years later the frequently quoted book of Argyris and Schön (1978) was published. Like March and Olsen, these authors also argued that actual learning processes in organizations seldom result in positively valued changes. Organizations seem to have problems in thinking and acting outside existing theories-in-use. In the following years many review articles were published analysing various publications on organizational learning (e.g. Dodgson, 1993, Fiol and Lyles 1985, Hedberg 1981, Huber 1991).

All these and other efforts notwithstanding, there is still a need for more scientific understanding on how to explicate actual organizational learning processes

(Thatchenkery 1996). The concept makes analysis difficult. For example, the traditional behaviouristic approach to learning seems to be problematic when applied to organizational learning. The stimulus-response sequence, traditional to the behaviouristic approach, is difficult to unravel as the combination of same stimulus, different response is rare in organizations (Weick 1991). Organizations are too routine-based to follow this traditional learning sequence (Leavitt and March 1988). Also, organizations do not provide the optimal (experimental) research site to unravel stimulus-response sequences. Moreover, researchers have problems *seeing* organizations and likewise seeing the learning of organizations, If organizations cannot be perceived, than it will be difficult to theorize about them, let alone about the process of organizational learning (Sandelands and Srivatsan 1993, Yanow 2000). Many researchers also have difficulty differentiating between individual and organizational learning. Argyris and Schön (1978) for example talk about organizations while in fact they are dealing with learning individuals within organizations.

In this book a broad definition of learning is used that emphasizes organizational knowledge construction: "Organizational learning is the process through which an organization constructs knowledge or reconstructs existing knowledge"[3]. The focus is on collective knowledge construction and is in line with more recent contributions to the organizational learning research stream (e.g. Brown and Duguid 1991, Cook and Yanow 1993, Elkjaer 1999, Gherardi 2000, Gherardi et al 1998, Huysman 2000, Nicolini and Meznar 1995, Pentland 1995).

Those who perceive organizational learning as a process of (re)constructing organizational knowledge have all been inspired by the social constructivist approach to knowledge development (Berger and Luckman 1966, Gergen 1994, Schutz 1971). According to the social constructivist approach, organizational learning is seen as an institutionalizing process through which individual knowledge becomes organizational knowledge. Institutionalization is the process whereby practices become sufficiently regular and continuous collective practices as to be described as institutions. The focus is on the process through which individual or local knowledge is transformed into collective knowledge as well as the process through which this socially constructed knowledge influences, and is part of, local knowledge. With organizational or collective knowledge, reference is made to knowledge as in rules, procedures, strategies, activities, technologies, conditions, paradigms, terms of reference, etc. around which organizations are constructed and through which they operate (Leavitt and March 1988). It is important that the organizational knowledge is capable of surviving a considerable turnover in individual actors.

Organizational knowledge refers to knowledge which an individual uses when acting as an organizational member. Much has been published about the concept of organizational knowledge, although there still seems to be confusion about its meaning.

First, organizational knowledge may be seen as residing in formal descriptions of the organization and its activities or in the retained records of organizational activity. This type of organizational knowledge consists of formal knowledge about the organization and may be viewed as analogous to the contents of an organizational knowledge base. Examples of such formal organizational knowledge are the formal record of organizational activity held in the minutes of meetings, company reports, organizational mission statements, financial information used in management accounting systems, organizational charts, etc.

Rather then knowledge *about* the organization, organizational knowledge can also be considered as being the knowledge *of* the organization. Morgan (1986) for example discusses this viewpoint when dealing with the image of a brain. Together with Ramirez (1983), he talks of organizations as holographic systems in which organizational knowledge may be embedded in their every component. With the growing popularity of organizational learning, this idea of an 'organizational memory' has become a subject of increased interest (Moorman and Miner 1998, Sandelands and Stablein 1987, Stein 1995, Stein and Zwass 1995, Walsh and Ungson 1991). The concept is somewhat similar to the sociological conception of a collective mind which as a construct evolved from the work of Durkheim at the end of the nineteenth century. However, whereas the collective mind refers to shared understanding and shared interpretation, organizational memory does not necessarily achieve the same end. Current literature on the topic has a rather functional approach to the idea (Stein and Zwass 1995).

The operationalization of the concept is restricted to organizational memory that allows for the acquisition, retention, maintenance, search and retrieval of information, leaving less structured organizational knowledge untouched. Organizational war stories, informal rules and routines, etc. cannot easily be collected, retained and retrieved. Not only is most of this knowledge tacit, but it is also frequently tainted by subjective interpretation and political bias (Orr 1990). The concept of 'organizational routines' (Levitt and March 1988, Nelson and Winter 1982) provides a possible solution to this problem of too formal an image of organizational knowledge. In their words:

> "The generic term 'routines' includes the forms, rules, procedures, conventions, strategies, and technologies around which organizations are constructed and through which they operate. It also includes the structures of beliefs, frameworks, paradigms, codes, cultures, and knowledge that buttress, elaborate, and contradict the formal routines. Routines are independent of the individual actors who execute them and are capable of surviving a considerable turnover in individual actors" (Levitt and March 1988, p. 320).

Besides constructing knowledge from within, knowledge can also be gained by adapting to the environment. This process of learning from other organizations takes shape by reacting to feedback information from the environment or by assimilating knowledge from other organizations. Organizational learning happens when this external knowledge is institutionalized within the organization.

Given the empirical nature of this book, we will also desist from delving any deeper into external learning processes. Instead, the box below will provide a brief synopsis of external learning processes. Failing to give adequate attention to the issue of supporting knowledge-sharing processes with the outside world has obvious implications for knowledge management. Chapter 8 looks at this weak spot in more detail.

External learning

During personal interactions, individual knowledge becomes collective knowledge while this knowledge in turn influences subsequent individual learning. As such, learning can be depicted as taking shape within a closed circle (see figure 2). Of course, in real life this circle is never closed. Organizational members are always influenced by knowledge from sources other than the organization (Weick 1991). Consequently, learning in the form of institutionalizing information should include processes of adapting to external knowledge. Basically, adapting to external knowledge happens in two ways: by reacting to information given in the form of feedback and by learning from the experiences of other organizations.

Learning by reacting to feedback information occurs when organizations learn from their own experiences by reacting to feedback information (e.g. Argyris and Schon 1978, March and Olson 1976, Senge 1992). This feedback information can be derived, for example, from customers responding to product quality and price, students responding to curricula, and citizens responding to social experiments. Hence, feedback learning requires communication with the environment and can occur through feedback instruments or through less formalized forms of communication. Examples are consumer research, opportunities for public comment, and policy evaluation. Another way to gain new knowledge is by learning from the experiences of others (Leavitt and March, 1988). This learning takes place, for example, through gatekeepers and boundary spanners (Aldrich and Herker 1977), through hiring newcomers (Huysman 2000), through inter-organizational cooperation (Powell et al, 1996), and through outsourcing, benchmarking and consultants (Leavitt and March 1988).

In the rest of this book we will not discriminate between internal and external learning but will mainly focus on internal learning as a manifestation of organizational learning.

3. THE PROCESS OF INSTITUTIONALIZING KNOWLEDGE

The essence of organizational learning is the (re)construction of organizational knowledge such as organizational norms, procedures, technologies, stories etc. Through knowledge-sharing, individual knowledge may become collective (organizational) knowledge while this accumulated knowledge will in turn influence subsequent action. In other words: organizational learning can be looked upon as a process that occurs as a result of the actions of the organization's members. These same actions are simultaneously influenced by collectively accepted knowledge as laid down in the norms and values, rules and procedures, and systems, that is by existing organizational knowledge. As a result of this duality between, on the one hand, the actions of individuals and, on the other hand, the deterministic or formative influences of existing organizational factors, organizational learning can be viewed as a process of institutionalization (Berger and Luckman 1966).

The term 'institutions' is used to describe social practices that are regularly and continuously repeated, are sanctioned and maintained by social norms and have a major significance in the social structure (Abercrombie et al 1984).

The notion of institutionalization
Different schools of sociology treat the concept of insitutionalization in different ways. For example, functionalists tend to see institutions as fulfilling the needs of individuals or society (e.g. Durkheim 1978, Parsons 1960) while phenomenologists may concentrate on the way in which people create or adapt institutions rather than merely respond to them (Berger and Luckman 1966, Schutz 1971). Institutionalization is the process through which social practices become sufficiently regular and continuous as to be described as institutions. The concept is widely used in sociology, though often without precise specification.

Scott (1987) distinguishes different 'institutional schools': two dealing with the process of institutionalization and two with institutions as systems. Institutionalization can be conceived of as 'a process of instilling value'. Selzneck, for example, argues that 'institutionalization is to infuse with value beyond the technical requirement of the task at hand' (Selznick, 1957, p. 17) which may lead to an unplanned and unintended nature of institutions. Institutionalization can also be conceived of as 'a process of creating reality'. Social order is founded on a shared social reality, which is created by social interaction.

Berger and Luckman (1966) describe the process of institutionalization as consisting of three phases or 'moments': 'externalization, objectification, and internalization'. These three moments have proven relevant when analysing organizational learning processes (Huysman 2000, Pentland 1998) and thus can help us to understand knowledge-sharing processes better.

Externalizing refers to the process through which personal knowledge is exchanged with others. Objectifying refers to the process through which society becomes an objective reality. During internalizing, "the objectified social world is retrojected into consciousness in the course of socialization".

As such, the authors point to a dialectical relationship between action and structure:

> "The relationship between man, the producer, and the social world, his product, is and remains a dialectical one. That is, man (not, of course, in isolation but in his collectivity) and his social world interact with each other. The product acts back upon the producer" (Berger and Luckman 1966, p. 78)[4].

Relating these processes of institutionalization with organizational learning makes it possible to analyse organizational learning as consisting of these three consecutive moments:

- *externalizing* individual knowledge in such a way that individually held knowledge becomes communicated;

- *objectifying* this knowledge into organizational knowledge so that shared knowledge is eventually taken for granted;

- *internalizing* this organizational knowledge among members of the organization.

After the publication of a book by Nonaka and Takeuchi (1995) it was no longer possible to talk unequivocally about externalization and internalization processes. The fact is that Nonaka and Takeuchi refer to other processes than those mentioned by the social constructivists. For example, when Nonaka and Takeuchi use the term 'externalization', they mean the process through which knowledge is converted from tacit to explicit knowledge; and when they use the term 'internalization' they are referring to the transfer from explicit to implicit knowledge. During the internalization and externalization processes as distinguished by Berger and Luckman and other authors, this knowledge conversion might also take place, but this does not have to be the rule *per se.*

The word 'objectify' has also been given an alternative meaning, which makes it rather confusing when used. Objectification is often looked upon as the process through which knowledge is recorded in, for example, reports and systems. However, in Berger and Luckman's treatment of the word this does not necessarily have to be the case. Knowledge can be collectively accepted without ever having to be recorded somewhere. Consider, for example, the culture of the organization.

Due to the possible confusion with the terminology, we have employed the following terms:

- externalization: exchanging knowledge (for reuse or renewal)

- objectification: collective acceptance of knowledge

- internalization: acquiring organizational knowledge.

Figure 2. The process of institutionalization with respect to organizational learning processes.

3.1 Internalization: acquiring organizational knowledge

When individuals acquire an organization's knowledge this is called 'internalization'. It is through internalization that individuals become members of the organization and remain so. In fact, internalization means the process through which one becomes an 'insider'. Acquiring knowledge takes place, for example, with the use of knowledge systems, training sessions, manuals, etc. But it is also supported by the transfer of organizational knowledge that has not been recorded. Spender (1996) refers to this social knowledge which is of a tacit nature, as 'collective knowledge'. A powerful way to support the transfer of this knowledge is by telling stories or swapping anecdotes (Sims, 2000). Another way is by letting people work together. There is a growing band of authors who argue that learning should be considered as being inextricably bound up with working (e.g. Brown and Duguid 1991, Gherardi 2000, Nicoloni and Meznar 1995, Yanow 2000). For example, Lave and Wenger (1991) introduced the concept of 'legitimate peripheral participation' as a method of learning by actively participating as opposed to learning outside the relevant task environment such as accumulating information from manuals.

'Learners need legitimate access to the periphery of communication - to computer mail, to formal and informal meetings, to telephone conversations, etc. and, of course to war stories. They pick up invaluable know how - not just information but also manner and technique - from being on the periphery of competent practitioners going about their business' (Brown and Duguid 1991, p. 50).

3.2 Externalization: reuse or renewal

Knowledge exchange takes place between individuals. Individuals share their knowledge with other people in the organization and this in turn begets shared knowledge. During the process of externalization personal knowledge is transferred to others. Externalization can take place in different ways; via formal channels such as meetings and project groups as well as through informal channels such as conversations in the corridors. Besides direct personal contact, externalization is supported by communication technology such as the telephone, intranet applications, and pen and paper.

The externalization of individual knowledge is facilitated when the knowledge is explicit by nature. Knowledge that can be expressed in language is only the tip of the iceberg (Polanyi 1958). Knowledge can vary in the extent to which it can or cannot be passed on. Almost all knowledge has an explicit and an implicit or 'tacit' dimension. Explicit knowledge can be conveyed with the help of formal, systematic language. Implicit or 'tacit' knowledge is not formalized and extremely personal and therefore difficult to pass on. That personal knowledge is often highly implicit gives rise to obstructions in the externalization process, which in turn can lead to substandard learning processes (Nonaka and Takeuchi, 1995).

Broadly speaking, there are two reasons why knowledge is externalized: knowledge exchange for the sake of reusing existing knowledge and knowledge exchange for the benefit of knowledge development. When knowledge is reused this involves knowledge 'flowing' from the knowledge carrier to the knowledge receiver. In the case of knowledge development it is not so much a case of one-way traffic but rather a reciprocal process of knowledge exchange.

Knowledge reuse involves an adaptive learning process. However, if too much attention is given to this adaptation in isolation, then conservatism or even inflexibility might result (Leonard 1996). In the literature on how organizations learn, this dichotomy between adaptation and innovation is often mentioned, albeit as a contrast between 'single loop learning' and 'double loop learning' (Argyris and Schön, 1978), 'adaptive learning' and 'generative learning' (Senge 1992), or 'exploitation' and 'exploration' (March 1991). In every case, in the first learning method existing knowledge is adapted in such a way that it remains unaffected. The second learning method involves renewing this knowledge.

3.3   Objectification

Just because knowledge is exchanged does not mean that the shared knowledge has already been collectively accepted. In other words, shared knowledge only turns into organizational knowledge when it is accepted as such by the organization's members. This process of collective acceptance or objectification does not always takes place consciously and can be a long, drawn-out process.

Collectively accepting local knowledge is the process through which the collective – often gradually – starts to accept existing shared knowledge as being part of the organization. This process is not so much one of sharing knowledge but more one of sedimentation. Von Krogh et al (2000) refer to this process in the context of knowledge creation as 'globalizing local knowledge'. For example, a group of technicians might have learned a new way of fixing a machine. This new operational knowledge remains local knowledge until it is accepted by the organization, for example as expressed in organizational stories, in manuals and in the training of newcomers. This process of objectification usually takes much longer than is the case with the three knowledge-sharing processes discussed above (Berger and Luckman 1966, Dixon 2000, Douglas 1987).

Because of its time-consuming and highly implicit nature, we did not include it initially in the empirical research. Nevertheless, our research revealed that ignoring the importance of collective acceptance can be a serious obstacle to organizational learning. In fact, most organizations in the research tended to ignore the outcomes of local knowledge-sharing processes or had problems collectively accepting these outcomes. The fact that knowledge-sharing often does not contribute to learning at the organizational level has important implications that we will discuss throughout the book and in more detail in chapters 8 and 10.

An example of an inflexible objectifying process
Brown and Duguid (1991) argue that inflexibility in an organization is often the result of managers not paying any attention to creative (group-)learning processes. During their day-to-day activities, individuals who interact with each other continuously create new knowledge as a solution to daily problems. They create new ways of working, give new interpretations to their situation and discuss existing practices. In other words, whereas externalization practices can be highly innovative, the problem often lies in inflexible objectifying processes, as new individual knowledge is often not transformed into new organizational knowledge.

Ethnographic research into the daily activities of repairmen at Rank Xerox (Orr 1990), for example, illustrated that during interactions people learn in highly creative ways. During training sessions, repairmen internalized organizational practices, all of which were described in manuals. The general organizational rule they were supposed to learn was that manuals should be used when diagnosing technical disturbances and that if the problem persisted, the photocopying machine should be replaced with a new one. The informal practices however were quite different: there was an unspoken rule that replacing a photocopying machine was a sign of one's own technical incompetence. Consequently, repairmen were highly motivated to fix technical disturbances to avoid being perceived as incompetent. If they were unable to do this on their own, they contacted each other for help in diagnosing the problems. This newly created knowledge concerning solutions to new problems was subsequently exchanged with others.

The problem was, however, that this knowledge remained informal and 'situated'; management remained ignorant of these creative learning processes. In other words, this newly communicated knowledge did not transform into organizational knowledge. Taking this story as an illustrative lesson for successful learning, it implies that learning organizations should be more aware of the learning that is taking place during daily activities. As various researchers have empirically illustrated, it is often during these day-to-day work-processes that new knowledge is created, leading to organizational improvement and renewal (e.g. Brown and Duguid 1991, Ciborra and Lanzara 1994, Cook and Yanow 1993, Easterby-Smith et al. 1998, Elkjaer 1999, Weick and Roberts 1993).

More often than not, collective acceptance occurs when knowledge-sharing processes are ratified through the endorsement of dominant coalitions within an organization (March and Simon 1993). By addressing the role of dominant coalitions in supporting knowledge-sharing, we include the notion of power in the discussion on knowledge management. Power plays a crucial role during the objectifying process. Dominant coalitions are formed by, for example, management, a critical mass, reference groups, old-timers, or charismatic personalities. Dominant coalitions can have a negative impact on the result of learning processes. For example, management - as an important member of a dominant coalition - might be oblivious to what is actually going on within the organization. By not accepting existing knowledge as being important to the organization as a whole, management hinders the construction of organizational learning. As a result the learning process of the organization will eventually become out of step with the learning process of individuals within the organization (Brown and Duguid 1991). An example of the power enjoyed by dominant coalitions that could frustrate the collective acceptance process is given in the box below.

The role of power in objectifying knowledge
A group of information system (IS) designers worked in the computer department of a large organization for a number of years. They all had a long service record within the company, where they had previously been employed as computer programmers. The company was using a number of routines that had been introduced by these employees over

the years. In this situation, the employees worked mainly on their own, there was little contact with the clients, almost every designer used his or her own particular style of IS design and there was a heavy bias towards technical details. The fact that their clients were not happy with these routines was not explicitly discussed at the time.

This complacency was reinforced because the department enjoyed a monopoly within the organization. The demand for information systems doubled at the beginning of the 1990s which resulted in a drastic expansion in the number of personnel. Twenty new system designers were brought in from outside the organization, all of whom had enjoyed a professional training in IS design and had often worked for a substantial length of time for software houses. These newcomers brought knowledge and skills with them that radically differed from the organization's existing in-house knowledge and skills. However, despite the fact that knowledge was exchanged, the existing collective routines and practices did not change because a critical mass consisting of 'old-timers' and management did not support the new practices. The majority of the newcomers eventually adapted to the established rules of the organization. Although they realized that clients were not happy with the methods and knowledge that were being used, they learned not to express their opinions in public and definitely not to report them to management.

Knowledge-sharing only supports the process of organizational learning when the different practices are followed by collective acceptance or rather knowledge objectification. Collective acceptance as a process is, in other words, the link between individual learning and organizational learning.

4. THREE TYPES OF KNOWLEDGE-SHARING

The various processes that in combination make up organizational learning processes, can be visualized using a knowledge-sharing cycle (see figure 3). The cycle provides a simplified picture of knowledge-sharing in organizations and is intended to help analyse the management of knowledge-sharing.

In this book, we take the point that learning processes can be supported by various knowledge-sharing processes: internalization by knowledge gathering and externalization by knowledge exchange (for the purpose of reuse or creation). Objectification takes place as part of these knowledge-sharing processes but at a much slower pace.

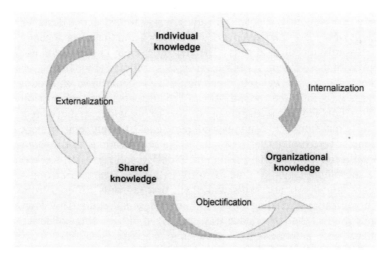

Figure 3. The knowledge sharing cycle

Internalization, or the process of learning from the organization, takes place by acquiring organizational knowledge. Externalization refers to the process of learning from other organizational participants. Internalization results in a growth of individual knowledge. Externalization results in shared knowledge. Depending on the process of externalization, this knowledge can take the form of reused knowledge or new knowledge. When knowledge is exchanged with the primary purpose of using it again, we refer to this as reusing knowledge. When knowledge is exchanged with the purpose of renewing it or in order to generate new knowledge we call this knowledge development. Table 3 summarizes these conceptual distinctions. It should be noted that distinctions are only conceptually relevant. In practice, knowledge-sharing can take various forms at the same time.

In this book we will concentrate on the three basic types of knowledge-sharing that can be derived from the knowledge-sharing cycle (figure 3):

— Knowledge acquisition as a result of internalization or learning from the organization. This process relates to individual learning.

— Knowledge exchange as a result of externalization or learning from individuals in order to reuse knowledge. This process also relates to individual learning.

— Knowledge development as a result of externalization or learning with individuals in order to develop knowledge. This process relates to group learning.

Table 3. Organizational learning and knowledge-sharing

Learning process	Learning from	Resulting in	Type of knowledge-sharing support
Internalizing	Organizational knowledge	Individual knowledge	Knowledge acquisition
Externalizing	Individual knowledge	Shared knowledge	Knowledge exchange (for purpose of reuse or development)
Objectifying	Shared knowledge	Organizational knowledge	All types of knowledge-sharing

As mentioned earlier, learning at the level of the organization only takes place when the collective treats knowledge as being organizational knowledge, that is, when knowledge has become collectively accepted and used. Collectively accepting knowledge is of strategic importance. Organizations who want to exploit internal knowledge-sharing should pay particular attention to the collective acceptance of shared knowledge. This process is – or rather should be – an integral aspect of the other three knowledge-sharing processes. In other words, we will discuss collective acceptance in the various chapters accordingly instead of in a separate chapter.

The three types of knowledge-sharing will be discussed in three separate chapters with illustrations from various practices. Chapter 3 describes situations in which knowledge is shared between individuals and the organization for the purpose of knowledge acquisition. This will be illustrated using practices at NN, Railways, and the Postbank. Chapter 4 presents situations at Cap Gemini, the Schiphol Airport, ING Barings and IBM where knowledge is exchanged for reuse. Finally, Chapter 5 discusses situations where knowledge is exchanged in order to create knowledge. These knowledge development processes will be highlighted with the help of actual situations that occurred at Stork, the Ministry of Housing and Unilever.

5. INFORMATION AND COMMUNICATION TECHNOLOGY (ICT)

Knowledge-sharing processes not only discriminate between the learning processes they support, but also in terms of the way in which the various processes can be supported by ICT (Hansen et al, 1999, Zack 1999).

Supporting knowledge retrieval or acquisition is mainly needed to enable the knowledge transfer between the organization and the individual. For this purpose, stored knowledge in for example reports, databases and knowledge bases is most appropriate (Zack 1999).

The role of ICT in supporting knowledge exchange for the purpose of reuse between individuals is often said to reside in the domain of electronic networks (Choo et al 2000). Intranets and Lotus Notes tools are the best known and are often referred to in this context (Ciborra 1996). Facilitating knowledge creation also requires the support of networks, although they are far less structured than is the case with knowledge-sharing for reuse. Often it is difficult to decide *a priori* which knowledge should flow between which members, and what the outcome or even purpose of networking would be. In this respect, networks are more like the communities of practices described by e.g. Brown and Duguid (1992). In some instances, GroupWare technology and electronic communities can facilitate the process of knowledge creation.

Table 4 presents the primary purpose of managing knowledge-sharing related to the type of learning, the type of ICT application they used to support the knowledge-sharing activities, and the various companies where we studied knowledge-sharing initiatives.

Table 4. Three types of knowledge-sharing

Types of knowledge-sharing	Knowledge acquisition	Knowledge reuse	Knowledge creation
Learning from:	Organizational knowledge	Individual knowledge	Community knowledge
Main purpose	Store dispersed collective knowledge to enhance individual learning	Prevent occurrence of knowledge gaps and redundancy	Combining knowledge to create new ideas and insights
(ICT) support	Knowledge bases	Knowledge bases and networks	Networks
Companies studied	• Netherlands Railways • National Netherlands • Postbank's Call Centre	• Cap Gemini • IBM • ING Barings • Schiphol	• Unilever R&D • Stork • Ministry of Housing

Given the empirical style of this book, not every potential ICT application that could support knowledge-sharing will be discussed fully. Despite our attempt to encompass as broad an area as possible of knowledge-sharing practices, several ICT applications have been underexposed. This applies, for example, to video-conferencing, extranet applications, group decision support systems, portals and e-mail. These technologies will only be referred to in passing.

6. SUMMARY

This chapter introduced some theoretical ideas surrounding the concept of 'organizational learning'. We believe the concept offers a good framework that can be of help when analysing knowledge-sharing. When we focus attention on learning by the organization, instead of just learning by the individual, knowledge-sharing is then also given meaning for the organization as a whole. Depending on the learning process, knowledge-sharing takes on different forms. Knowledge acquisition occurs when individuals learn from organizational knowledge. Knowledge exchange takes place when individuals learn from each other. Knowledge development occurs when individuals learn *with* each other. ICT can support and facilitate these three knowledge-sharing processes in different ways. In part two of the book the three forms of knowledge-sharing with the help of ICT are discussed in more detail.

PART 2

PRACTICES OF KNOWLEDGE-SHARING

The three types or purposes of knowledge-sharing - knowledge acquisition, knowledge reuse and knowledge development - reflect the sequence of the practices of knowledge-sharing that we discuss in this part of the book. Ten different case studies that tell us about various aspects of knowledge-sharing are described and discussed.

Chapter 4 describes situations in which *knowledge acquisition* plays a role. The key question is how individuals actually learn from their organization. We are concerned here with the process of acquiring knowledge at the individual level. The following organizations are examined: Postbank VKS, the insurance company NN, and Netherlands Railways.

Chapter 5 provides examples of *knowledge reuse.* We begin by focussing mainly on how individuals learn from each other and proceed to analyse ways in which knowledge exchange is channelled through personal or technical networks. The companies examined in this chapter include Schiphol Airport, ING Barings, Cap Gemini and IBM.

Finally, chapter 6 concentrates on practical examples of how individuals share knowledge for the purpose of *knowledge development.* We explore the question of how individuals can learn together in order to create new knowledge that will ultimately be beneficial to both the organization and the individual alike. Unilever, Stork and the Ministry of Housing are discussed with regard to this.

While it is true that some companies do have markedly more ambitious goals than discussed here, these were still very much at the early stages of development. As mentioned earlier, we will mainly focus on the practical experiences that organizations gained from managing learning processes. We have therefore taken the current *status quo* as our starting point and examine the way in which the learning process evolves and how ICT applications are used with regard to each individual case. All three chapters primarily centre on the practices of knowledge-sharing. We will discuss each illustration of knowledge-sharing separately. Every case will end with a reflection on the positive and negative aspects of each initiative. Part three will focus more attention on the analysis and discussion of the successes and failures related to all the knowledge-sharing initiatives discussed in part 2.

CHAPTER 4

KNOWLEDGE ACQUISITION:

Knowledge-sharing with the organization as the knowledge provider

1. INTRODUCTION

The Claims department of the 'National Netherlands' (NN) insurance company, the Sales and Customer Services division of the 'Postbank', and the Travel business unit of the Netherlands Railways all have one thing in common: they structure knowledge-sharing in order to provide individuals with access to organizational knowledge. The goal of knowledge-sharing in these cases is to acquire knowledge for the purpose of using it in operational day-to-day work processes. Learning takes place on the individual level: the individual learns from the organization. The employees do not provide any added value to the company either through the knowledge that they possess or have internalized. That is not to say that these people are uneducated. On the contrary, in order to perform their tasks well secondary or even tertiary level education is an important requirement.

However, the area of knowledge that they have to master has been neatly arranged in such a way that the internal transfer of knowledge from the organization to the individual is quite sufficient. Knowledge database systems and intranets are the selected methods for transferring knowledge here. We have grouped the cases in this chapter under the common term of knowledge acquisition: the act of making the explicit knowledge of an organization available in order to turn it into the tacit knowledge of an individual. We have called this learning process in chapter 3, 'internalization'; the transfer of knowledge within the company to individual employees.

Internalization frequently entails the socialization of employees: how a company allows an employee to operate within the existing culture and how it ensures that the employee conducts business well within the boundaries of the company's norms and values. The first steps towards realizing this are taken as early as the employee selection procedure.

Internalization is also the process of transforming explicit knowledge into an organization's tacit knowledge (Nonaka and Takeuchi 1994). It takes place on two levels: the new knowledge that an organization creates and the knowledge at the level of the individual. Employees have an active role to play in the learning process in creating knowledge and developing their own personal skills in order to perform tasks. The use of structured methods and systems such as knowledge databases, manuals and training courses also contributes to this process of acquiring organizational knowledge. In this chapter we focus in particular on this latter interpretation, that is knowledge acquisition as a form of knowledge internalization.

In organizations whose daily tasks are carried out using routine procedures collective knowledge is often explicitly formulated knowledge. The bulk of this knowledge can be digitized and made available through information systems. The desire to make knowledge explicit goes hand in hand with the desire to store knowledge. Therefore databases and workflow-systems are typical applications selected by these organizations (Hansen 1999). Document-management systems are also popular in connection with this. In addition, systems are currently being developed that are geared more towards 'human management', i.e. supporting people in the execution of a daily task (Blackler 1998). In order to make effective use of collective knowledge, a lot of attention has been given to data mining and data warehousing in the last few years.

Of the three companies discussed here, National Netherlands is the only one that actually talks about knowledge management. In fact, the term only came into fashion there after a consultant had pointed out to National Netherlands that it was, in fact, engaging in the practice of knowledge management.

1.1   Knowledge acquisition in practice

The practical examples given in this chapter all demonstrate a strong tradition in capturing knowledge, whereby knowledge is made available to employees. Because of their own specific organizational characteristics and market positions, each company tends to value knowledge in a different way and has also found its own solution. The Postbank, for example, talks about its Infobank while NN offers the same sort of function, yet refers to it as its 'knowledge base'. Indeed, the Netherlands Railways discusses knowledge management behind the scenes, but certainly does not yet see its information channels as an opportunity for knowledge gathering.

Linking up an information or knowledge database to a learning environment is an interesting example of how organizational learning can work in practice. At both NN and the Postbank the 'knowledge base' fulfils an important role in educating newcomers.

The common thread running through the companies that we have grouped under knowledge acquisition is that they are all large, bureaucratic organizations that have recently gone through a major reorganization process. Moreover, the two companies from the financial service sector both made the jump from being product-driven organizations to becoming market-driven organizations. The problems and solutions that they have chosen are strikingly similar. Both companies opted for a knowledge database system. However, while NN proceeded to create an organizational structure around its knowledge database system, the Postbank opted for a less formalised approach.

The reorganization at NN and the Postbank resulted in employees no longer having to deal with customers concerning one specific subject, but having to be knowledgeable about a wide range of products instead. A clear division has been created between the front and back office at the Postbank. The front office continued under the name Sales and Customer Service (VKS), and became a public help-desk providing information and advice on savings. NN brought people from different product groups together and placed them in teams that began operating with a much stronger focus on the different regions. At the Railways the relationship between the reorganization and the knowledge initiative is more vague.

The companies make use of different ICT applications. However, the knowledge database system at NN and the Postbank are comparable with one another: they both use a standard application with graphic features where the user can click on to the correct documents. Similarly, both organizations have developed plans to link the knowledge databases to the intranet. The Railways differ somewhat in that it uses a mobile device with a knowledge database system that is primarily meant for employees who are constantly on the move. The following sections describe the different case studies in greater detail.

2. POSTBANK SAVINGS: KNOWLEDGE-SHARING WITHIN A CALL CENTRE

Profile of the Postbank

With approximately seven million account holders, the Postbank is one of the largest financial service providers in the Netherlands. Paying by giro is one important aspect of the service. Through the giro, the Postbank offers a wide range of services in the areas of payments, savings, loans, shares, insurance and mortgages. One business component of the Postbank is the Postbank Savings division. About four years ago, Postbank Savings made the transition from a product-driven organization to a market-driven organization, at which point the front-desk and back office activities were divided. Neither group has any product specialization. The front-office works as a call centre and is called "Sales and Customer Services" (VKS). A coordinating centre is responsible for planning and staffing the groups and managing the knowledge database.

There is a reasonably large turnover of staff. On average, they remain with the Sales and Customer Service department for two to three years. A hard core of staff who are 'Postbankers' in heart and soul, work alongside them. One-hundred-and-eighty people work at VKS, divided into ten groups under the leadership of the department head. VKS is primarily geared towards providing customer-service. Customers' enquiries are usually about depositing money, opening accounts, withdrawing credit and closing accounts. In addition to this, there are also enquiries as a result of periodic special offers on savings. Special offers are an important method of attracting new customers or retaining customer loyalty. These are almost always accompanied by advertising campaigns, for the duration of which VKS staff must be well informed about the special offers currently available.

The daily tasks of employees at the Sales and Customer Service Department consist of answering customers' enquiries. An average employee starts working at the department upon completing his or her college education and most leave after three years. Newcomers start with a one-week training course that lasts for four weeks in total, where they learn about the Postbank's different savings products through an interactive learning system. In addition, they receive training in how to interact with customers.

One of the employees told us:

> 'The question and answer game was hard in the beginning, however, I was able to use the Infobank, which I'd learned to work with during my training course, for many of the questions. The Postbank has a 'clean desk policy'. We are not allowed to use any other type of reports, so we must answer the customer using the computer. This was certainly irritating in the beginning whenever a computer problem cropped up, but after six months you can answer practically any question off the top of your head. You could say that I could answer eighty percent of the questions straight away; I use the Infobank for the remaining twenty percent. The eighty percent mostly have to do with standard procedures such as how to open an account or set up a deposit account, how to make payments and how to close an account'.

The employees' main priority is to provide the customer with the correct answer to his or her particular enquiry. They can rely on the Infobank to provide answers to almost all the enquiries made. Here they will find information on both current and past offers and current interest rates, as well as information on competitors' products and interest rates. Furthermore, they can use the system to call up information on account holders. These customer profiles provide an up-to-date overview. If they cannot find the answer instantly, or if knowledge about a specific administrative procedure is required, they either ask an immediate colleague or one of the specialists or another colleague who has been especially appointed to shuttle back and forth between the front and back office to help with unusual issues. What is useful, is that they receive electronic memos containing information about new offers or important issues for VKS:

'I begin each day by reading the memo. Up until just recently, we were often better informed than management but now they too have access to the Infobank. In fact, all my colleagues use the Infobank intensively. This enables our team leader to see how we answer enquiries, both from a social perspective as well as with regard to the accuracy of the answer we give. The key factor is that we give the customer a satisfactory answer.

2.1 The knowledge initiative

By creating a division between the front-desk and back office, knowledge from the back office needed to be made available to the staff at the Sales and Customer Services (VKS) department who were manning the telephones. This could be achieved by providing training on product content and by creating an information base. It was also necessary for the information to be up-to-date.

The most powerful argument for creating a knowledge database was to make knowledge accessible in the workplace combined with the execution of a 'clean desk' policy. This knowledge database focuses on making information available so that the Call Centre can perform its daily duties and newcomers can internalize the knowledge. The system frees staff from having to depend on knowledge and experts and puts them in a position where they are able to solve customers' problems, thereby increasing customer satisfaction. The system also replaces the traditional processes of sharing knowledge. Most of the information contained in the Infobank is of a stable nature: the information relates primarily to product content. The information about special offers stems mainly from other departments within the company. The Infobank must ensure that the staff no longer need to possess technical knowledge about the savings products. Two employees with higher vocational training, or even tertiary education, are involved in the upkeep of the system. These employees are the knowledge brokers behind the knowledge database.

The knowledge database replaced an older information system at VKS. Every bit of knowledge available about the products was placed in the knowledge database. This consisted not only of information that could be found in the manuals but also knowledge that employees had in their heads. 'Mind-mapping' techniques were used here while mainly old-timers were approached for providing the input.

Preventing the knowledge from becoming obsolete is an important focal point. The two employees from the coordinating centre play an important role in this. Their knowledge broker role is supported by their position in the social networks within the company. Having good personal contacts with the marketing department and with the other departments ensures that they receive the right information at the right time. VKS must also be quick off the mark when something goes wrong in the handling process. A social network plays a crucial role here too. The knowledge database is inadequate to cope with situations in which there are rapid changes or acute problems. For technical reasons, it takes at least one day to incorporate changes in the Infobank. Whenever such situations arise, face-to-face communication as well as methods such as memos or notices are used to inform employees.

Although the Infobank is important for the day-to-day work, Postbank Savings could survive for several days should the Infobank become inaccessible. The organization is not totally dependent on the Infobank as the staff have assimilated this knowledge during the process of carrying out their work.

New staff members at VKS are given training in knowledge of the savings branch and in other skills. Within one month they can perform on an operational level with ease and confidence and after six months they are familiar with the entire field.

> **Infobank**
> The knowledge within the Infobank reduces training time. The Infobank is linked to the Postbank's learning environment, which is an interactive training programme. In light of the nature of the activities taking place, it is important that the staff members are trained in specific skills. The front office staff have a commercial approach. Mentors, who walk around at the call centre, supervise newcomers. Direction is given primarily through the department heads. They listen in on conversations or recorded conversations in order to help staff members develop their skills and knowledge. It is precisely because this knowledge is barely visible that particular attention is given to the level of discipline with which it is used.

The users are satisfied with the system. They are very proficient at responding to complaints, despite not being required to have far-reaching knowledge of the savings products. At the moment, the system does not enable employees to give any direct feedback about the complaints or questions raised by customers. However, steps are being taken to improve the call code system and the (customer)complaint registration system.

2.2   Experiences

Postbank VKS is a good example of an organization concerned with making knowledge collectively available to individual employees, through which individual employees in particular can learn from the organization. Although the organization now functions as the knowledge provider, in an earlier phase, through 'mind-mapping', the transfer of knowledge from the individual to the organization took place. Employees now possess collective knowledge about the savings branch, which they have assimilated through an interactive learning environment. At the Postbank we see in particular how knowledge databases contribute to the effectiveness of organizations that operate according to fixed routines and how valuable explicit knowledge is to this type of company.

The importance of routine knowledge is relatively high and easy to formalize. VKS avoids heavyweight terms such as 'knowledge management' and 'organizational learning'. The employees are not knowledge carriers, but rather knowledge vehicles. They translate information to answer specific customer enquiries.

An important learning experience at the Postbank is that it has successfully married the requirements of the company with those of the individual employee. Linking up a knowledge database to a training environment has further facilitated the internalization of knowledge on an individual level. However, even though a system to register complaints does exist, there is little evidence that any systematic learning from customers takes place

Enablers
- organizational change
- clean desk (the removal of alternatives)
- training on the job
- integral part of the operational process
- support from management

Potential risks
- geared towards 'reacting to' rather than 'learning from' the customer
- strong emphasis on *individual* learning

3. NATIONAL NETHERLANDS: KNOWLEDGE DATABASE PLUS PERSONAL NETWORKS

At the National Netherlands (NN) insurance company, structured knowledge sharing has been going on for some time, without it actually being referred to as knowledge management. The organization can be compared to the Postbank in different ways. Firstly, both organizations focus on the knowledge that staff members need to carry out their daily work. Secondly, the knowledge base at NN also has an encyclopaedic quality and plays a supporting role in individual learning processes.

In a number of other respects, NN in fact differs quite significantly from the Postbank. Postbank VKS operates as a call centre geared towards providing a swift service, while NN has staff members who have long service records and who have already absorbed a great deal of the knowledge contained in the knowledge database system.

Profile of National Netherlands
National Netherlands (NN) is part of the ING group. NN owns an insurance company specializing in claims as well as a life insurance

company, which has recently merged into one single company. NN also works through its distribution channels with insurance agents.

Until 1994, the Claims department was split up into a number of divisions such as fire, cars, transport and liabilities. Each division had its own department staff. Knowledge was present in the form of guidelines, the practical knowledge of the employees and specialist knowledge possessed mainly by employees with long service records.

NN works primarily with insurance brokers. Employees at these brokers were using products from the entire organization. This meant that they either had to deal with a vast number of counters or that they were unable to make sufficient use of combinations of insurance packages. From a commercial point of view, it was more attractive for NN to change from being a product-driven organization to a market-driven organization.

The insurance company is structured on a regional basis, whereby teams of employees would come to operate within different districts. The teams were no longer responsible for one product, but for all the products and services offered. This has helped to significantly reduce the number of counters. Henceforth agents simply came to the same counter. NN distinguished itself through its employees' long service records and its high level of knowledge. A market survey revealed that this makes NN stand out among its competitors. It is precisely because of its recognition of the importance of knowledge that NN invested heavily in storing knowledge after its reorganization. It has consciously tried to make knowledge independent of the individual via a knowledge database system.

NN was one of the first organizations to go public with its knowledge database system (Den Hartog and Huizinga 1997). Knowledge is recorded in a knowledge database that is accessible through the network. It enables employees operating in teams to cover different categories of products. Alongside this, an organizational structure has been set up consisting of specialists, coordinators and contact people who all play a role in the knowledge-sharing process.

3.1   The knowledge initiative

When the outline of the new organization became clear, NN grew anxious about how it could safeguard its distinguishing assets from being exploited by its competitors. The question was therefore raised: What happened to the knowledge within the organization? In 1994, the company started a knowledge storage circuit. Knowledge was stored by recording knowledge about products, prices and regulatory procedures. Alongside this, contextual information was also incorporated such as information about specific types of insurance buyers.

NN's Knowledge database system

The knowledge database system is a formal way of recording knowledge, and includes elements such as gathering existing knowledge, creating accessibility through the establishment of an automated system, maintaining and updating the system and establishing procedures to reflect information requirements. Employees can then help customers from behind their computer screens which significantly reduces the waiting time. The knowledge database system has to be serviced on a regular basis as information becomes obsolete very quickly and keeping it up-to-date requires a lot of effort.

The knowledge database system now forms part of the company's main operational process and it is therefore impossible to imagine the organization without it. Many of the instruction manuals have disappeared and knowledge is now only maintained in the knowledge database system. It is also an important training tool for new staff members. At the same time, people admit that not much will happen if the computers crash. The staff has enough tacit knowledge to work without using the system.

Alongside the knowledge database system, NN has created a knowledge network with knowledge brokers based on official roles. NN distinguishes between three different knowledge broker roles: the knowledge coordinator, the specialist and the contact person. Through this formal social network, the organization has created the possibility for individual employees to learn from other individuals. It also makes individuals responsible for keeping knowledge up-to-date. This responsibility rests mainly with the knowledge coordinator and the specialist.

The position of *knowledge coordinator* is a full-time job. It represents a staff function within the insurance divisions. This staff member is responsible for the upkeep of a specific area of knowledge, for generating new knowledge and for passing on knowledge to the different districts. The coordinators have an initiating and motivating role with regard to the specialists. They also provide input to product development from the perspective of their own subject area. The risk with this job is that it could end up as a hotchpotch of all sorts of activities.

The *knowledge specialist* specializes in a specific field. Specialists work in the different regions and are part of the team. They act as walking encyclopaedias for their colleagues and provide support to the knowledge coordinator. Originally, the specialist' was part of a team doing similar work to his or her colleagues. However, this conflicts with the responsibility for keeping up-to-date with the area of expertise. The position is therefore currently filled based on 'being a specialist' and the role of claims processor has subsequently become less prominent.

The *contact person* works within a team. He/she is an experienced employee who is required to focus on a specific group of products. The contact person acts as an expert for colleagues and the team leader. It is not a separate task but is looked upon instead as part of the job. If they prove themselves suitable, the contact person will eventually be considered for the role of specialist.

With this structured network, NN attempts to give substance to the idea that 'knowledge must flow'. A communication structure, in which regular discussions take place, formalizes the knowledge flow. Taking minutes of the meetings and procedures so that reports can be distributed shapes the formalization process even further. Alongside this, it is clear who can be approached from within the team. The Quality office coordinates the supervision of the quality of knowledge storage. Management insisted on a centralized coordination process. The Quality office also monitors the knowledge database system and the relationship between the knowledge storage circuits and the external technical staff.

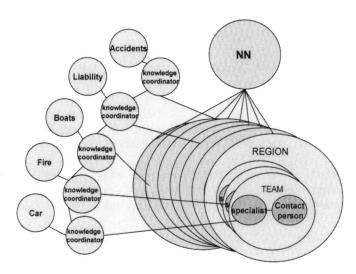

Figure 4. Example of a network at NN

3.2   Experiences

Knowledge exchange and knowledge storage were borne out of necessity at NN. It sprang from the realization that the company would lose an important lead when dramatically changing its organizational structure.

The knowledge database system and the knowledge storage circuit with its underlying communication structure needed to guarantee a continuous flow of knowledge. Realizing this blueprint in practice was much trickier. Staff tended to react with scepticism to the concept of knowledge management. Knowledge storage was introduced under the theme 'knowledge must flow' at the same time that a massive reorganization was taking place. Side by side with a traditional hierarchical organization, a functional structure for storing knowledge emerged. At this point, some people fell within the hierarchical framework, while knowledge coordinators found themselves on the outside. Due to this, knowledge coordinators had very little influence over the specialists' input. In practice it appeared that the knowledge coordinators and the specialists jointly took care of gathering knowledge on a specific area. One problem during the specialists' appointment process was that they were first selected according to their knowledge of a particular field. However, having knowledge about a specific subject does not necessarily guarantee that people also have the social skills that are necessary for working within a team.

The tasks of the specialists include keeping the knowledge database system up-to-date, training new employees and keeping abreast of case law. Changes to the knowledge database system should also therefore be discussed with the specialist. Contact persons draw attention to the policy within their districts with which specialists can proceed further. Although roles are rigidly defined, in practice they can always cause tension with regard to time management, especially if work pressures are high.

The functions of the knowledge database system and the specialist complement each other. The knowledge database system offers answers to many questions, although a great deal of it is already internalized. For answers to specific questions, employees mainly rely on the specialist. One reason for relying more on the knowledge broker than on the knowledge database system is that many questions deal with exceptions to the rules which are generally not stored in the knowledge database system. For example, if there are a lot of questions about claims as a result of excessive snow problems caused by avalanches, the knowledge database system draws a blank. Moreover, a knowledge database system does not help in determining the type of social skills that should be employed: how people should deal with particular customers, enquiries or complaints. For this, they seek help from more experienced people.

An important lesson is that it is very much in the interests of an organization dominated by routine processes to combine a technical solution with the creation of an organizational network. Knowledge exchange at NN flows through the networks of knowledge brokers. They represent the chain to the other employees. This combination of a technical and social-organizational network enables NN not only to improve the learning process of individuals but also to learn as an organization. Through the roles of knowledge brokers, individual knowledge becomes collective knowledge. One obstacle in this process is the mix-up of responsibilities, namely for the specialists. They are part of a team and yet at the same time also responsible for sharing knowledge. These responsibilities do not always dovetail with one another.

Another drawback is that with the present form of knowledge-sharing, NN hardly learns anything from its customers. In this respect, it can be likened to the Postbank.

In the meantime, NN Claims and NN Life Insurance have now merged into one single entity. Knowledge database systems are currently being developed for those parts of the organization that have not yet had access to them and knowledge workers have been appointed. NN has learned its lesson from earlier initiatives and now applies this to the selection process for knowledge workers. When specialists are selected more attention is now given to assessing their social skills. Management concerns itself with knowledge management - the term is now being used - but the extent to which knowledge-sharing really thrives among the personnel is still unclear.

Enablers
- change in the organization
- need to store knowledge
- part of the service
- organizational solutions combined with technical solutions
- disappearance of manuals
- support from top management

Potential risks
- confusion about roles
- wrong selection criteria for knowledge brokers
- keeping the knowledge database system up-to-date
- not learning from customers

4. THE RAILPOCKET, THE MOBILE KNOWLEDGE SYSTEM OF THE RAILWAYS

Until 1996, most conductors walked through the train carrying huge bags containing the instruction manuals and the railroad timetable. The sheer weight of the bags regularly led to complaints among the conductors. Much has changed since the arrival of the Railpocket.

For a number of years now, conductors have had access to the 'Railpocket', a mobile, pocket-sized computer that contains all the information they need to carry out their daily work. At the beginning of the shift the conductor loads the latest information from a disk, while reports on how the trains have been operating can be read at the end of the shift. Reports of acts of aggression, for example, are much more readily available from the process manager who in turn can react more directly.

Profile of the Netherlands Railways
The Railways now operates as a holding with independent business units. The core of the company is made up of the business unit Travel, the business unit Stations and the business unit Real Estate. The

Railways has gone through a number of major reorganizations. An important segment of the personnel at Netherlands Railways Travel consists of mobile personnel, such as conductors and engine-drivers.

Before the shift starts, conductors collect a diskette containing information issued by the Railways. By putting the diskette into their Railpockets the conductors are informed about the latest train details. The conductor also keys in administrative data about the train into the Railpocket. This concerns reports of anything out of the ordinary (cleanliness, delays, defects on the line and to the train, wrong trains (sidecars), reports of aggressive behaviour and sales on the train).

The Railpocket is not used as a means of sharing knowledge among conductors. In general, conductors did not feel that there was a need for this. For the most part, a strong sense of operating independently prevailed among the conductors. They are responsible for a certain route, together with the engine-driver and occasionally another conductor. People who apply for the job of conductor have a predisposition towards acting independently and providing a service, they are not team players. As one of the conductors remarked:

> 'We don't know who else is in the system or who is getting on the train after us. On the few occasions that we do meet, we mainly swap stories in the cafeteria. Of course, you eventually figure out that certain routes are more likely to have fights on them than others.'

The key advantage is that all sorts of information is now available, not just travel information, but also information about procedures. According to one conductor, this also represents one of the risks:

> 'Should such a device break down for some reason, then you have to fall back on your own experience and knowledge. Because of the fact that you hardly ever have to rely on this now, you are actually less equipped to carry out your job.'

NS Railpocket
Railpockets have been in use for a number of years now among the 3000 conductors. The Railpocket is a mobile computer containing information about procedures, travel information, and information about repairs. It also has the capacity for keying in reports: a mobile knowledge database system. Although this device is not actually used for knowledge management purposes, its role can be compared to that of other knowledge database systems described earlier such as the Postbank Infobank. The Railways has made the organizational knowledge that was recorded in instruction manuals available via the Railpocket. Individual conductors can gather knowledge in this way.

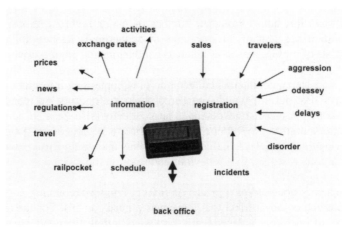

Figure 5. Schematic representation of the functionality of the Railpocket

4.1   The knowledge initiative

The Railpocket is the initiative of a conductor who developed the device in his spare time. Initially, he developed a software programme that could process braking distances. Originally, conductors had to work out braking distance times for every train ride. Because he was also fed up with having to cart kilos of manuals and other paperwork around with him, he created databases that took over most of the paperwork. The first device contained the travel planner, a system to work out breaking distance times and a calculator to work out foreign exchange rates.

The idea was quickly taken on board by the conductor's boss and a trial was launched in the south of the Netherlands. The trial was a runaway success and the conductors did not want to part with the device. Following the trial, a project group was set up that has now been transformed into a management group. Since then many more data files have been added to the Railpocket. It contains transport information, information about work duties, and information about procedures. The device is small in scope which is also one of the most important limitations with regard to adding new applications. It does not (yet) contain communication capabilities and extras, such as purchasing tickets, have not (yet) been incorporated[5].

Originally, the information was one-sided. However, for some years now the Railpocket can also register information such as train administration. This information is fed through the Railpocket and read into the data warehouse at the end of the shift. Most of the information is made available in the form of management information to the production manager in charge of the conductors.

The Railpocket only has a limited role with regard to this. Conductors reveal more personal experiences during group sessions or through individual feedback.

4.2   Experiences

Conductors are still hindered by the limited amount of space available to fill in information. The Railpocket chiefly provides rapid information and gives quicker feedback to the conductors. The device is not yet suitable for up-to-the-minute information. For example, conductors are often no wiser than the passengers regarding the reasons for a train delay. The Railpocket helps the conductors perform their duties. That does not yet make it a means of exchanging knowledge with one another: informal contacts are still more important in this respect. It is, however, a means of making organizational information available to a mobile group of employees.

Knowledge management at the Railways is still, in many areas, at the conceptual stage. The operational knowledge at the Railways is not subject to frequent changes. Much of what is now called knowledge management was formerly known as information management. One of the most valuable lessons learned during the introduction of the Railpocket was the fact that this tool forms an intrinsic link between a practical problem and a pragmatic solution. A second lesson is that the potential for knowledge exchange has still not been exploited.

Enablers
- fulfils an immediate need
- support from management
- bottom-up initiative

Potential risks
- limited applications
- limited knowledge exchange
- limited use for production managers

5. DISCUSSION: THE ORGANIZATION AS KNOWLEDGE PROVIDER

In the case studies given in this chapter the organization acts as the knowledge provider. This view seems to depart from traditional discussions about knowledge management. In many books on knowledge management and the design of knowledge-intensive companies, people play a crucial role in knowledge flows.

In this chapter we have discussed companies that base their knowledge-sharing practices on a stock approach to knowledge. The nature of the work is routine and geared towards providing a service. The most important interaction occurs with customers, not with colleagues. Therefore, staff are not managed based on their contribution to the knowledge-sharing process but rather in relation to their customer-friendly behaviour. This usually takes place using standard management principles. Table 5 gives an overview of the features of a knowledge acquisition process, such as those that were discussed in the case studies in this chapter.

Table 5. Features of practical situations

Learning process	Postbank	NN	Netherlands Railways
Objective	To capture, mind-map and update knowledge with an eye to becoming more customer friendly.	To consolidate the knowledge build-up in relation to the transition from a product-driven to a market-driven enterprise.	To simplify operations.
ICT	Infobank	Knowledge system	Railpocket (mobile knowledge system)
ICT's role	Supportive, used regularly, provides a learning environment.	Supportive, used regularly.	Supportive, used.
Type of learning process	Capturing knowledge, subject-specific knowledge through training on the job; linking practice with learning.	Capturing knowledge, Integration of subject knowledge, Individual learning and personal networking.	Providing support to mobile personnel during the execution of their tasks.
Support for the learning process	Knowledge bases and interactive learning environment.	Knowledge bases, Organized network.	Knowledge bases.
Worker profile	Sales employee	Office and knowledge worker	Mobile worker
A selection of experiences	No feedback, increases speed at which tasks are carried out	Friction between hierarchical and functional responsibility	Dependency, no management of knowledge

It is difficult to talk about successful knowledge-sharing here. The initiatives are successful in that they complement certain organizational goals. At the same time, they are also unsuccessful in that they fail to exploit the full potential of knowledge-sharing. The Railpocket is successful because it satisfies a specific need of the employees. This also applies, to a certain extent, to the employees of NN and the

Postbank. Furthermore, it does not seem to matter whether the initiative comes from the top or bottom, although in all cases support from top management is vital.

ICT and knowledge database systems
In the different examples of the case studies given, information and knowledge are entrenched in operational practices. ICT plays an important role in practice. This is important in the sense that without ICT the process of knowledge-sharing would look very different, colleagues would not be able to work as efficiently and customers would have to put up with a longer waiting time for their questions to be answered. Knowledge database systems, therefore, apparently do contribute to the effectiveness of a company, although organizations make no attempt to quantify this.

What stands out in these cases is the fact that the ICT-application is securely embedded in the normal work processes. In this type of knowledge-sharing, knowledge database systems play a supporting role with regard to customer service. This support is principally geared toward the individual employee. In terms of organizational learning processes, these businesses stimulate individual learning in particular. Only NN manages, through its personal networks, to successfully make knowledge collective too. The question remains whether every organization wishes to learn from knowledge-sharing. This need is probably less of a priority in routine operating organizations. We will discuss this aspect of learning in more detail in chapter eight.

Knowledge databases appear to be well suited to work environments where short and flexible terms of employment prevail. When staff are employed for a long time, they have a tendency to internalize the knowledge anyway and make it their own. Similarly, a knowledge database system can offer valuable support to employees who either have to work independently or who are often on the move. The knowledge in the knowledge database system has to have a certain level of stability in order to maintain its up-to-date value.

Knowledge work and the knowledge worker
Intuitively, these examples appeal less to one's imagination as the work is not immediately perceived as being knowledge work, either by the employees themselves or by outsiders. We can ask ourselves whether this is a result of the nature of the work, the nature of the knowledge or the nature of the knowledge worker.

It is not easy to generalize about the staff employed at the different organizations. How can you compare a conductor with an insurance agent? What is clear is that people do not rush to describe themselves as knowledge workers. Rather, they see themselves as taking part in routine, service-driven work or as a small cog in an administrative production process. The companies are very much service-driven and this means that the staff must either already possess specific (social) skills or else develop them.

The different organizations scarcely perceive their own initiatives as examples of knowledge management. To some extent it is therefore perhaps wrong to judge these initiatives in that way. It is only at NN that one can talk about an explicit entrenchment of the knowledge streams within the company. Within this organization, a clear distinction is made between the knowledge workers who have formal roles and the office staff who are mainly customer-driven. The people who are not directly involved in any formal role in knowledge management are the ones who are the most critical of its benefits[6].

Learning by acquiring knowledge
The companies we studied all considered it very important that their employees learned from the organization. Capturing knowledge plays an important role in this respect. An employee would use the knowledge in a situational context. Individual learning does occur, but collective learning takes place even less frequently.

At NN the goal is much more to share knowledge through organizational networks and this is why NN has succeeded in incorporating different forms of learning in its knowledge-sharing process. At NN the personally structured networks appear to fulfil an important role, certainly during moments when critical questions are asked. The development and dissemination of knowledge take place through the interaction of specialists and coordinators and other members within the organization. Personnel are more likely to look for the answer to a question through the personal networks than through the data files on a technical network. Furthermore, there seems to be some tension surrounding the operational tasks of specialists related to their functional teams and the tasks that they have to perform in relation to the knowledge management initiative. In addition, the regional divisions also appear to represent an obstacle to the effective exchange of knowledge between the specialists.

The other companies are very good at supporting individual learning processes. Individuals are mainly stimulated to use the organization's knowledge to perform their daily tasks. Mainly because of the relatively stable information with which these companies are concerned, the knowledge databases seem to fulfil their roles admirably. A new phenomenon here is one of dependence: people are placing less trust in their own knowledge and experience because data is present in a coded format. The different companies also fail to exploit opportunities. Few companies take advantage of the possibilities of learning from their customers and there are hardly any inducements to use the knowledge and experience of individual staff members.

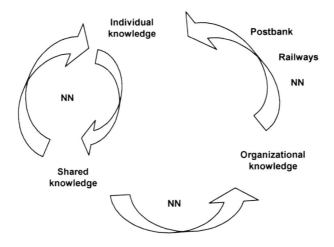

Figure 6. Learning processes in practice

6. SUMMARY

In this chapter we discussed the practical aspects of knowledge acquisition in three companies: NN, The Netherlands Railways and the Postbank. The case studies shared a number of common features with one another. In all cases, knowledge-sharing concerned the acquisition of collective knowledge by individuals. These individual learning processes occurred in somewhat routine situations. All the ICT-applications were introduced for the preservation and use of organizational knowledge. The process of gathering collective knowledge is mainly channelled through knowledge database systems. This type of ICT support is ideally suited to relatively routine, independent work. The cases are also distinguished by their emphasis on individual learning. Only NN offers an example of collective learning. By facilitating the existence of personal networks alongside the knowledge database systems, and by appointing knowledge-brokers, NN ensures that everyone can reap the fruits of the results of this learning process.

CHAPTER 5

KNOWLEDGE REUSE:

Knowledge-sharing with the individual as the knowledge provider

1. INTRODUCTION

For many companies reuse of knowledge is considered to be an important objective in order to get knowledge management initiatives off the ground. The aim of these companies is to let people learn from one another. To avoid situations where people are constantly reinventing the wheel it is better to record the knowledge of in-house experts and disseminate it further throughout the company. This way, consultants can solve problems much more quickly and pass this information on to their clients. Reusing information and not reinventing the wheel are frequently heard arguments. For this purpose, companies create both social and technical networks in order to stimulate knowledge exchange.

We present four case studies in this chapter. We will examine how these different companies put this type of learning into practice and will look at the problems they encounter. All four companies in this chapter are service providers, albeit in different industries. They use their organizational and technical networks in different ways. The results of the learning processes are also different for each organization.

Externalization, or the exchange of individual knowledge, plays a central role in this chapter. This can involve the exchange of tacit or explicit knowledge. According to Polanyi (1958) knowledge has two dimensions:

- Explicit knowledge that can be passed on using formal, systematic language.

- Tacit knowledge that is very personal and difficult to put into words.

It is easier to externalize individual knowledge if this knowledge is explicit. However, knowledge that can be expressed in words is only the tip of the iceberg (Polanyi 1958). When individual knowledge is expressed in language it becomes communicated or shared knowledge. This knowledge is often subsequently recorded in specific data files that might be accessible to other organizational members via, for example, an intranet. Many western companies consider this form of converting the tacit dimension of knowledge to explicit knowledge to be one of the main objectives of knowledge management (Nonaka and Takeuchi 1995)

Broadly speaking, there are two reasons for externalization: knowledge exchange in order to reuse it and knowledge exchange for further knowledge development.

Reuse is a matter of knowledge flowing from the knowledge holder to the knowledge recipient. During this process, individuals learn from each other. Whereas with knowledge development it is not so much a case of one-way traffic, but rather a reciprocal process. In this situation individuals do not learn *from* each other but *with* each other. Reusing knowledge is a learning process that boils down to adjusting and adapting knowledge. In contrast, knowledge development involves a renewed learning process. In this chapter we focus in particular on knowledge reuse, while knowledge development is discussed in Chapter 6.

Knowledge is made accessible to the organization through structured networks, often in the form of intranets. Project-driven organizations in particular are grateful for the opportunity to use intra- and extranets. An intranet can offer a wide range of different uses. It can make procedures, manuals and information about standard formats accessible. It can offer news groups within a company or support competence areas within a company (Choo et al 2000).

In knowledge-driven consultancy companies the internal network is often just as important as the external network. It is in the employees' own interests to make use of the intranet as increased visibility often results in more interesting assignments and projects being offered.

1.1.   Knowledge reuse in practice

This chapter revolves around the key question of how individuals exchange knowledge with each other for reuse purposes. In many cases this takes place through a technical or organizational network in which people within the company have the opportunity to codify their knowledge. The type of network very much depends on features such as the identity of those initiating the knowledge exchange within the organization, organizational characteristics such as geographical distribution, the structure of the organization (teams, project groups, etc.), the need to work together and the employee's interests. In practice we therefore encounter a wide variety of situations. In this chapter we will discuss the networks at the Airport, Cap Gemini, IBM and ING Barings.

The importance of ICT at Amsterdam Airport Schiphol is relatively limited. However, intranets mean a great deal to ICT-companies such as Cap Gemini and IBM. At ING too, the intranet is a way of facilitating the exchange of individual knowledge. But alongside the technical networks, we also encountered the importance of personal networks as a means to exchange knowledge.

2. STRATEGY-DRIVEN KNOWLEDGE-SHARING: AMSTERDAM AIRPORT SCHIPHOL

Strictly speaking, Amsterdam Airport Schiphol fails to meet our selection criteria. While it is indeed true that there is a wealth of experience and Schiphol does use ICT, nevertheless knowledge exchange does not actually occur on a routine basis. In fact, the knowledge management project at Schiphol ran for two years and has now been stopped. Nevertheless, we decided to include it here as its 'knowledge centre' provides an interesting example of support for knowledge reuse.

The initiative mainly focussed on the knowledge worker within the company with the intention of stimulating knowledge exchange and knowledge reuse among employees. The knowledge centre played a central part in this. The core of the employees consists of personnel who play a role in policy development and service provision to foreign airports. The knowledge centre plays a part in this transformation by recording the available knowledge and making existing documentation and expertise accessible to others for the purpose of reusing it.

Amsterdam Airport Schiphol encountered certain obstacles that we will identify at the end of the case description.

> **Profile of Amsterdam Schiphol Airport**
> Amsterdam Airport Schiphol is the administrative and operating company responsible for the operation of premises and sites belonging to Schiphol airport. The organization consists of 1750 people. The average age of people working there is 44. The organization has gone through two reorganizations within a very short period. At the end of the nineties the 'transfer to the future' was implemented. In this instance, Schiphol saw itself as a knowledge-driven organization.
> Quantitative growth is not an option for Schiphol. Growth will be primarily qualitative, for example with regard to international advice on how to furnish airport premises. Knowledge is an important production factor here. The knowledge initiative also fits in with this.

2.1 The knowledge initiative

The knowledge management project consists of three phases:
- Phase 1 Knowledge at the press of a button
- Phase 2 Knowledge for one another
- Phase 3 Knowledge in motion

Schiphol started its knowledge initiative from scratch. A good documentation facility did not exist. The establishment of a knowledge centre was especially geared towards finding information and making it both available and accessible. This concerned personal reports and documents. By gathering this documentation the knowledge centre also gained an insight into where expertise within Schiphol was located.

The first year was used mainly to build up the documentation facility. The knowledge centre is meant to be an oracle for various questions concerning contents that are aimed internally as well as externally. Questions that focus on internal issues often have a reference function: who is responsible for a particular procedure, which projects are underway, who is responsible for the various projects, etc.

Given that Schiphol has to deal with an ageing workforce, the preservation of knowledge is an important objective. This consists of recording the expertise with regard to content and harnessing the personal networks and contacts that people have built up. Schiphol recognizes the importance of knowledge in particular with regard to product innovation (selling knowledge to other airports, international cooperation) and improving internal procedures.

There is hardly any question of organizational entrenchment in this phase. Seven people were directly involved in the project, the majority of whom worked at the knowledge centre. Aside from the project leader, a database specialist from Schiphol also worked on this initiative. In addition, people with a library science and documentation background were involved.

A typical product of the knowledge centre includes a document with a web-compass, document compass or knowledge compass.
–   a document compass refers the user to the relevant literature;
–   a web compass refers the user to important home pages;
–   a knowledge compass refers the user to in-house or external expertise.
In addition, the knowledge centre keeps a record of the information requests and responses.

The initiative also supports departments that wish to have a better-structured database to make the acquired knowledge available to the knowledge centre. It is especially geared toward the information and documentation aspect: this involves making codified knowledge in particular available. The knowledge management initiative was at the transition point between the first and second phase.

The initiative has existed since 1997 and coincided with a change in direction for Schiphol when the board emphasized the knowledge intensity of the company. The board gave the project its seal of approval for a three year period. At the end of the year 2000, the project ended. The board decided not to continue with the initiative.

Knowledge reuse in practice

The knowledge centre had 350 regular users, which was 60 to 70 percent of the target group. A survey carried out among the employees revealed that next to the managers, policy makers in particular used the knowledge centre. They were satisfied with the quality, the expertise and the timeliness of the product. The survey also showed that the more frequently employees used the knowledge centre, the more satisfied they became. Although the knowledge centre met the information needs of the personnel, there was some irritation about the level of precision insisted upon when formulating an enquiry.

Using ICT

ICT-use did not yet have a prominent place in Schiphol's knowledge management initiative. Because the project leader shared offices with the intranet coordinator they could continuously exchange ideas. Intranet is one of the activities that had been brought under the auspices of the communications group. A number of applications were predicted that could be important in the second phase which was called 'Knowledge for one another'. This included GroupWise, an e-mail system, a document management system and Telpage. Telpage is a 'Yellow pages' system. A knowledge card is situated behind the name and address of each employee on the intranet. The knowledge card can be used by individuals to fill in details of their respective areas of expertise as well as the projects in which they have participated. It also features a picture of the employee concerned. The process to incorporate the document management system into GroupWise suffered delays. It seemed that quite a few people were still very attached to their own systems.

2.2   Experiences

One feature of the Schiphol organization is that in some respects it is an organization with an 'ageing' workforce where people, so to speak, work on their own little islands. It took time to implement the exchange of documents. However, when people realized that the documents were handled with care and respect and that the information remained accessible to them, they were quite happy to make their reports available. The knowledge centre had to win their trust.

There is some resistance at Schiphol Airport towards pushing ahead with the digitization process. People will not venture out into the unknown of their own accord. They still read very little via their computer screens and remain doggedly attached to the printed medium. Another challenge for Schiphol rests in taking advantage of the existing personal networks. Although the company says it considers this to be important, there is still as yet no ready solution to transfer knowledge via these existing networks. Master-apprentice relationships are being considered as one possible option.

A more mundane problem for Schiphol is that it applies principles that would seem to be more appropriate in an organization carrying out routine-based operations.

Such organizations tend to focus primarily on developing 'stock' rather than stimulating knowledge exchange.

Enablers
- the initiative originates from the bottom-up
- top management support
- fits in with the process of strategic change
- change of strategic direction

Potential risks
- top management support
- ageing workforce, island culture
- fear of digitization

3. ING BARINGS: KNOWLEDGE SHARING BETWEEN COUNTRIES

At a recent conference it became apparent that successful examples of knowledge management occurred particularly in companies with a powerful mission, such as the World Bank and in companies with a wide geographical distribution. One of the case studies that fulfils the geographical distribution criteria is supplied by ING Barings.

Profile of ING Barings
ING Barings is an international investment bank and is part of the ING group with its head office in Amsterdam, the Netherlands. Over 9000 people are employed at ING Barings, and they are all distributed throughout more than fifty countries. Managing the knowledge throughout the fifty branches has always been heavily decentralized. Several years ago, partly because of the increased technological possibilities to stay connected globally, the board articulated the need to make ING Barings more transparent. In this sense it would, for example, be useful for an account manager in London, to see exactly what is happening in Budapest. Clients too would find this information useful.

3.1   The knowledge initiative

Due to the broad geographical distribution of its international branch offices, ING Barings personnel are often in the dark about the state of affairs and background of the branch offices in different countries. Consequently, an initiative was drawn up at the highest level to establish a world-wide intranet, as yet only among ING Barings employees, to facilitate the exchange of information about the different branch offices. The information consisted of recorded knowledge about the most prominent clients of the various international branch offices, the key products, the contact persons for the different products, the most talked about deals, a country's economic situation and relevant legislation and rules.

An Executive Committee member introduced this initiative in 1997. This meant that from the very outset the initiative had a sponsor at the highest level. Subsequently, a working group was put together comprising a Chair, a couple of ICT people and some trainees. This working group functioned for a time under the supervision of the sponsor, after which two more project leaders followed.

ING Barings Guide

The intranet at Barings makes knowledge and information from fifty Barings branch offices accessible. After one year of preparation, the project group decided to use a Lotus Notes Domino application and to call the intranet the ING Barings Guide. This Lotus Notes Domino application made it possible to make the knowledge available to everyone while it was being managed locally, that is to say the local knowledge was not stored or updated at a central point.

Local information managers store local knowledge by using an Internet browser via the internal network, in a central database. One major advantage is that this does not require any technical or ICT-related expertise. Logging information locally and the fact that ICT-expertise is not necessary to manage the knowledge are seen as huge plus-points of the application.

3.2   Experiences

One of the stumbling blocks which ING Barings ran into was how to mobilize knowledge in the different countries. It proved very difficult to identify a contact person to function as the local information manager (LIM). A good secretary or another - preferably senior - employee from the back office often proved to be the best person to act as the LIM. It was important to have a permanent contact person or LIM at every branch office. The problem at the large foreign branch offices was that many different people had to collate and acquire information.

Furthermore, it was hard to calculate just how far the information could be relied upon and how up-to-date it was. It also became apparent that it was very important to do a good PR job on the Guide. People had to be made aware of the value and necessity of developing and ultimately using the Guide. It was easier to mobilize people when they were more involved. However, in practice it transpired that many of the branch offices did not have a strong track record with regard to involving employees in the system. For example, there were instances where people changed positions, but forgot to sign out with the project leader of the Guide.

The best way to stimulate active involvement was by creating a critical mass. This critical mass only existed when the system contained a lot of relevant information that employees regularly needed, such as up-to-date information. In addition, the project leader discovered that mobilizing people was also important in order to avoid the emergence of different, decentralized initiatives. In this respect, many offices used the Internet instead of the Guide in order to promote their own interests. Mobilization did not stop as soon as the different branch offices had handed in their contributions. The project leader told us:

> 'It is an illusion to think that you can abandon the offices to their fate. Everything is managed from head office, you have to continuously exercise control; you have to keep on monitoring, maintaining contacts and checking information'.

The most troublesome aspect of mobilizing people was that the project leader had to constantly keep in touch with the different countries, via e-mail, video-conferencing or by telephone. It was therefore important to find a suitable medium and not badger people too often about keeping information up-to-date. One practical solution was to continuously come up with a new pretext to ring a branch office and then surreptitiously enquire about their contribution for the ING Barings Guide.

The lofty ambitions with which the project was launched certainly seemed to be a hindrance in the beginning. Initially, people looked upon the ING Barings Guide mainly as a technical diversion. It seemed very tempting at the beginning of such a system to exploit all the technical possibilities. This is a trap that many companies are in danger of falling into when they set about implementing an intranet. Because of this trap, the duration of the project got out of hand. ING Barings concluded from this that the system should be kept as simple as possible from the start by focussing on essential information categories. Another classic problem linked to this, was the risk of a lot of irrelevant information finding its way into the system. One of the causes of this is when the goal of the project is not clearly communicated to the end-users. It was vital for the LIMs to realize that people actually made use of their information. This helped to increase the likelihood that they would continue to maintain the system. Given that people only use information that is relevant, timely and reliable, it is important to ensure that only this type of information finds its way into the system.

Technology caused the usual problems. One major mistake was that the technical feasibility of the system was not tested out beforehand. For example, it was not possible to connect all the offices. For security reasons, ING Barings uses the Cita-system rather than a modem. Approximately ten out of 50 branch offices were not connected to the system, such as India and countries in Latin America. They were forced to send in their information by fax.

One negative incidental issue was the relatively bad economic situation in which ING Barings found itself at the end of 1998 and beginning of 1999. Reorganizations were going on and people were made redundant. It seems that an unfavourable economic climate is not conducive to initiating structured knowledge exchange. As the project leader put it:

> 'I had the feeling that I was on board the Titanic, in which case you really should not come forward with initiatives such as the ING Barings Guide'.

Despite these teething problems, on the whole ING Barings is positive about the ING Barings Guide. Recently all the countries were able to be reached and there is now a contact person at every office. Positive reactions from the different countries are also coming in.

Just as at Schiphol Airport, the ING Barings Guide initiative finds itself on the border between knowledge acquisition and reuse. We decided to present the cases as illustrations of knowledge reuse instead of acquisition because reuse of knowledge was the guiding principle that led to the introduction of both initiatives.

Enablers
- support from top management
- satisfy the need for transparency
- good PR for the intranet

Potential Risks
- focus on technical goals and solutions
- mobilizing people
- economic situation

4. CAP GEMINI'S MIXED NETWORKS

The average consultant at Cap Gemini spends most of his or her time with the customer. She communicates with her employer or colleagues via e-mail, mobile telephone or the intranet. Increasingly, Cap Gemini's intranet - labelled 'Galaxy' for the world-wide application and 'CapCom' for the national variant - is becoming accepted. A consultant who in the last year has had the role of knowledge manager reports:

> 'In principle, you can find just about everything on the intranet: you can use it to look for information or even to order your shopping. Before using the intranet we actually make a sort of pact with our employer that requires us to consult specific information sources once a week. The information is updated on a weekly basis. Three years ago the system almost expired. Nobody took responsibility for its content. The problem with CapCom was that it was far too bogged down with technical details. When you introduce an intranet you should not attempt to offer everything at once. It is precisely because of the work pressure that you should present everything as simply as possible. Often, only one tenth of the intranet's capacity is used'.

Profile of Cap Gemini
Cap Gemini is an international, knowledge-driven organization that aims to offer ICT-related organizational advice, to implement organizational change projects with and by clients and to provide services that take advantage of ICT. The Head Office is situated in Paris, France while the Head Office for the Netherlands is in Utrecht. Forty thousand people work for Cap Gemini world-wide, with about 7,500 in the Netherlands. Cap Gemini is first and foremost a software house that supports its clients during transition processes. Cap Gemini's system for charging for services is based on hourly declarations. Clients are usually given advice on a project basis. Cap Gemini is a decentralized organization; the authority to make decisions takes place low down in the organization. Three management levels can be distinguished: unit management, general management and the board. In addition, there are three operation levels: those implementing the project, the experts and the senior experts. The average age has risen in the last two years to 32.

Frequently used applications are the agenda and the 'mug-shot album'. The most frequented facilities are the simplest ones. The picture gallery in particular seems to be very useful, for example, to know what a colleague whom you are about to meet at a client's location looks like or because it helps in tracing the authors of the documents.

CapCom intranet
The knowledge management eye-catcher at Cap Gemini is the much talked about company intranet. Cap Gemini has two intranets that are linked to one another: Galaxy, which is the world-wide intranet and CapCom, which is the national network.
CapCom has already been in use for four years. Approximately 80 to 90 percent of the employees make use of CapCom, especially to follow news and developments within Cap Gemini and to obtain specific information about a division or unit. This is why, for example, a weekly average of 300 people read information from the business-unit Migration Services, while only 60 people actually work at the unit itself.
    CapCom is looked upon as a living organism or an anarchic system, in that it stands or falls depending on how much the employees contribute to it.
    CapCom was originally intended to reduce the amount of paper mail. After the network was launched, various expensive packages were purchased to create knowledge bases. In the long run these knowledge bases did not seem to make a difference. The knowledge bases proved too complex to search for simple documents. CapCom only really took off when its usefulness became obvious to the

personnel. Mail was placed on it, along with the agenda and a 'picture gallery' containing photographs of the personnel.

Yet still, not everyone is happy with the system, the search facility in particular leaves a lot to be desired. New projects like Sibylle should provide support to the search habits. Sibylle creates software clones of the current experts and should significantly increase the chances of finding the right document. This system was only launched recently.

CapCom is also frequently used to look up standards, for example guidelines on how to compile a report and to find specialists via the 'Yellow Pages'. In addition, the intranet contains a database of 'best practices'. In point of fact this consists of a database with final reports. An important element of 'best practices' is the quality system called 'Perform'. This is a collection of methods and techniques that can be used as a template to standardize the way in which projects are carried out world-wide which has been made accessible via the intranet. The storage of knowledge in the databases takes place on a voluntary basis and leaves a lot to be desired. In practice, it is difficult to stimulate people to publish their experiences on the intranet. People generally tend to use the intranet to acquire information and not so much for the sake of recycling knowledge.

There are also differences between the aspiration and the reality. The reference system does not (yet) function properly, as a knowledge manager informed us:

> 'It is important to be aware of who knows what and to approach the right person on the basis of this. You just cannot do this via a system, this type of thing works best through personal networks.'

In fact, using CapCom ought to be part of the daily routine, though the knowledge manager had to admit that he did not use the system very often in the days when he was still a consultant. That has certainly changed since he took on the role of knowledge manager. In 1997 knowledge managers were appointed to all the different divisions and it was their role to ensure that reused empirical knowledge was channelled in the right direction. The knowledge manager is formally required to take responsibility for stimulating knowledge exchange, such as via the intranet. However, in practice, the knowledge manager is more of a linchpin in the network, bringing people into contact with one another. Senior staff members in particular can direct others if they are stuck with a specific problem or question, or can tell them who can help them in person.

A knowledge manager described his position rather flippantly as an expensive telephonist. He continuously brings people in contact with one another: he has to know exactly what kind of knowledge can be found and where it can be found. The role of knowledge managers and their tasks is not clear enough among the employees; some employees are not even aware of the existence of this position.

This applies even more so to the new position of 'knowledge management champion'. The knowledge manager himself considers the term 'knowledge manager' an unfortunate one:

> 'I'm not the knowledge manager, the managers here are the knowledge managers, knowledge is in people's heads, they should manage their own knowledge. Managers can play a coaching role in this.'

4.1   The knowledge initiative

The knowledge intensity of the company and its high turnover forces Cap Gemini to focus a great deal of attention on what knowledge means to its organization. Knowledge intensity demands both specialist knowledge and a broad application of this knowledge. In addition, it is especially important that the experiences of individuals and the knowledge that they have acquired while carrying out projects for clients are made available to colleagues. This facilitates the reuse of knowledge. Through this, Cap Gemini can make great leaps forward in terms of efficiency, spurred on by the wishes of its clients.

The staff agree that the culture at Cap Gemini is especially open and - compared to other large consultancy firms - quite informal. Not everyone walks around in a business suit, colleagues are friendly with one another and quite a lot of knowledge-sharing takes place. A happy office is an important feature for Cap Gemini. Cap Gemini stimulates individualism with the slogan 'Master of your own destiny'. This means that employees are, in principle, responsible for their own future within the organization. At the same time, management stimulates collectivism. It considers it to be important that staff learn to network and create communities. Having 'Master of your own destiny' as a guiding principle has important repercussions for the daily practice of knowledge reuse. Given that the individual is now responsible for his or her own personal development, there is an intrinsic motivation to be continuously aware of what is happening inside and outside the organization; what is hot and what is not.

In connection with this, Cap Gemini has another general perspective: the importance of generalism in order to avoid too strong a specialism. This aspect of the organization's culture has consequences for the practice of knowledge exchange given that generalists are much more dependent on knowledge-sharing than specialists. A spin-off is that within Cap Gemini roles rather than positions are discussed. A role is temporary and can only be filled for six months to a year at the very most. Examples of roles include staff members of the implementation team, SAP specialists, programmers and project leaders. In addition to a change in job content, people employed at Cap Gemini must also be prepared to act as a boss in one project while reversing this role in another situation. This requires an open and tolerant disposition. Not everyone is suited to such flexibility. As a result of the importance of having your future in your own hands as well as the importance that

Cap Gemini attaches to generalists and flexibility, the organization invests heavily in the individual development of its employees. Cap Gemini employees are engaged in education and training courses both during the day and in the evenings.

On the whole, people arrive at Cap Gemini with little or no experience, while the majority are keen to progress to a senior adviser's position or management. For the first two years that someone is employed at the organization, particular attention is given to his or her broad development. In view of the fact that consultants work more on a project basis, it is possible to allow newcomers to collaborate on projects during the first few years in a kind of master-apprentice set-up. In most cases there is at least one senior staff member and one newcomer on a project team. It takes about six to eight years to become a senior.

Knowledge reuse in practice
Knowledge exchange for the purpose of knowledge reuse is important. Management propagates this message and consultants implement it in practice. Because of the open culture employees drop into each others' offices quite easily. People are prepared to help others and to relay their experiences. For some time now, Cap Gemini has included the extent to which people exchange knowledge with their colleagues in their performance evaluation. Teamwork and accessibility to others are considered to be of paramount importance. It rarely happens that people keep information to themselves. In other words: knowledge management in the context of supporting knowledge exchange practices is continuously taking place at Cap Gemini and is embedded in its culture. Examples of this can be found in the Special Interest Groups and the frequent conversations that take place in the corridors.

In addition to these informal initiatives for knowledge exchange, approximately five years ago, about the same time as CapCom was introduced, the board put forward a number of initiatives to systematically manage the reuse of empirical knowledge. Alongside the creation of knowledge management roles, the board increasingly stressed the need to record the experiences learned during the projects and disseminate these via the intranet.

This aspect has not (yet) had many repercussions in practice. By the time a project is approaching completion, the next project has already turned up. This demands a lot of discipline on the part of the project employee to pause and take stock of the experiences he or she has had and to write them down in the form of 'dos and don'ts'. This has more to do with an organizational block than a psychological block: in a commercial organization acquiring the next big project has greater priority than contributing to the knowledge reuse process.

Despite the fact that a great deal of knowledge exchange is going on, the term knowledge management is hardly ever used. The board has also recently started to view knowledge management as an important issue but at the same time considers it to be taking place on too much of a voluntary basis. In addition to creating knowledge broker positions and supporting the exchange of experiences, the board has since then considered giving more weight to an employee's contribution to CapCom in his or her performance evaluation.

Employees appear to attribute different interpretations to the concept of knowledge management or otherwise avoid using this explicit term. When asked for their opinion about the knowledge management policy at Cap Gemini, employees gave a mixed reaction. One business-unit manager said:

> 'That's a difficult one, you can't manage knowledge, it's all woven up in the organization and in the people, knowledge management is something that belongs to the individual, through courses and experience and suchlike.'

Another business-unit manager told us:

> 'Whenever I hear that term I envisage people writing down their experiences and throwing them into databases. You can't do that, you're not going to tell me that you can wade your way through a lengthy story and then think at the end of it that you've absorbed that experience, what nonsense!'

Knowledge development through personal networks
As well as the official knowledge management initiative, Cap Gemini acknowledges an unorganized (unstructured) knowledge-sharing process that exists in particular as a result of the individual's need to continue to develop knowledge. This process evolved bottom-up from the culture that made knowledge-sharing vital. The initiatives focus on exchanging experiences and developing new knowledge. This is how different Special Interest Groups (SIGs) were launched, membership of which is voluntary.

The SIGs focus on special themes or knowledge areas, such as ERP-software and e-commerce. SIGs bypass divisions and begin at an operational level. They are very popular at the moment due to the importance of further developing personal expertise. SIGs sometimes end up as Competence Centres that become embedded in the formal structure of a business unit.

Knowledge-sharing by way of swapping project experiences takes place both in conversations and through reports. These reports are in the form of a glossy brochure that is also suitable for external use. One impediment to sharing knowledge via brochures is the age-old rule that forbids clients from being referred to by name. These days the organization no longer observes this rule as rigidly as it used to. Should a client explicitly state that he or she wishes to remain anonymous, then written reports are only circulated in-house, via the 'for your eyes only' brochures. A verbal exchange of experiences is by far the most common practice. People know where to find one another be it during organized gatherings, in each other's rooms or in the corridor.

4.2   Experiences

Opinion is split at Cap Gemini with regard to the success of knowledge management. Classifications vary from 'good' to 'mediocre'. One reason for this is that knowledge management has so far been strongly associated with recording experiences which seems to have had little success up to now. Aside from the fact that people are generally not convinced of the need to do this, another important reason for this resistance is that consultants often cannot and will not be motivated to set down their experiences in a database once a project has been completed. Cap Gemini has therefore deliberately opted for a 'reward and punish' strategy (Van Grieken 1999). People get tit for tat if they ask for information that is available through Cap Gemini elsewhere and they are rewarded if they contribute knowledge. Given that business-units have a lot of influence at Cap Gemini and the fact that there are different viewpoints within these units concerning the usefulness of recording experiences, the policy hardly ever permeates down to the operational level.

Knowledge management was not given a high priority by senior management until the end of 1999. At that time the market was exceptionally favourable. Software houses do not have to operate in a highly efficient manner. Since last year knowledge management has had a sponsor within senior management. This has created new dilemmas. People, who want to stimulate interest in knowledge management from the shop floor, believe that its success lies in being unstructured. The upper echelons however want to establish solid rules and boundaries. Those whom we interviewed admit that knowledge management is an evolutionary process for which the organization still has to implement many changes. Cap Gemini is still embroiled in this process.

Cap Gemini has a culture and way of working together that strongly promotes knowledge-sharing in practice. Furthermore, senior management is prepared to invest in knowledge management. The involvement of senior management also brings a risk which we discuss in part three of this book as being part of the management trap. The pressure of time is an important problem when trying to realize the more formal initiatives, as hours spent outside the organization are valued more highly than contributions to in-house knowledge development.

A number of reasons can be given to explain why knowledge-sharing comes from the bottom-up. Within Cap Gemini, managers and consultants often end up at the unit level while knowledge management is in fact an organization-wide issue. Given that Cap Gemini is a very decentralized organization, it would be hard to implement knowledge management from the top down. Yet many people at the managerial level consider it vital to focus attention on the management of knowledge. This is also stimulated by the need to be service oriented. The client wants quick solutions to questions, thereby forcing knowledge to be recycled. Situations arise where colleagues are wandering around simultaneously within a client's organization without even realizing it, or in which Cap Gemini employees advise a client without taking previous prior experiences with that particular client into consideration. One person we interviewed told us:

'The client knows more about Cap Gemini than Cap Gemini knows about itself.'

Reuse is especially necessary because the very size of Cap Gemini means that the wheel is often being reinvented. Reusing knowledge can also go beyond division boundaries. Questions from clients can traverse these boundaries which requires a broad understanding of the client's subject area. The challenge for Cap Gemini lies in uniting these different needs. Management sees the solution in stimulating the reuse of knowledge and knowledge creation in specific areas. In addition, the large turnover of staff at Cap Gemini with 15 percent passing through makes it necessary for this knowledge to be recorded, otherwise it would be lost to the organization.

A balance does exist between the technical and social networks at Cap Gemini, even though it is less structured than, for example, at NN. On the one hand the organization has created formal roles, and on the other hand platforms for informal knowledge exchange and creation in the shape of SIGs also exist. The organization's open culture boosts knowledge-sharing in areas where the technical side does not work effectively.

Enablers
- support from senior management
- 'reward and punishment' strategy
- bottom-up initiative
- open culture and individualism
- personal need
- quicker solutions required
- clients' demands

Potential risks
- the pressure of time
- insufficient involvement of the existing culture
- thwarting initiatives (initiatives from the top down)
- decentralized structure and responsibility

5. KNOWLEDGE-SHARING AND KNOWLEDGE MEASUREMENT AT IBM

At IBM a world-wide initiative called Intellectual Capital Management (ICM) has been launched. The initiative consists of 49 competence networks and is the largest implementation of Lotus Notes and web technology in the world. Two years ago the system was awarded an international prize. In the Netherlands ICM began at IBM Global Services. The ICM project team considers its task to be to address the subject of knowledge management within IBM. The project team consists of eight people.

Of these, two of them work for the Netherlands and six for EMEA (Europe/Middle East/Africa). In addition, there are regional contact persons, who spend 10 to 20 percent of their time on ICM. These are, in a manner of speaking, ICM mentors. The contact persons are senior professionals from a specific knowledge area. ICM is further implemented according to the standard management practices of a business unit. The initiative has really taken hold in different countries: in the United States where a group focussed on the theory behind knowledge management, in the Netherlands through a consulting team and in England where a group of software developers identified a need to record and recycle software.

IBM tries with ICM to transform the knowledge of individual employees via the intranet into collective knowledge. Individual knowledge workers can use the knowledge in their daily work operations. Part of the transformation is a change in culture that has been implemented world-wide in the last few years. Having first chosen the clients to be their main focal point, every level within IBM has now become convinced that teamwork is one of the vehicles for realizing this. The focus on the new culture is primarily knowledge-driven, and centres on re-engineering (customer relations), procurement and intellectual capital.

Since Lou Gerstner took the helm at IBM, the company has been going through a major transformation. In the words of Ross Kanter (1990) it has become a dancing giant. During the nineties, IBM energetically focussed on reorganizing its core activities, switching from supplying hardware and services to offering services, consultancy and e-commerce. For this purpose, the company has heavily invested in exploiting and developing knowledge.

5.1 The knowledge initiative

IBM's strategy is to work efficiently with the available knowledge on a global scale, also with respect to its international teamwork. IBM recognizes the need to do this as competition is fierce. Employees are hard or even impossible to find and have to increase their work tempo to keep the clients satisfied. Furthermore, IBM can effectively deploy its employees and resources in this way.

ICM is a combination of problem-driven and opportunity-driven initiatives that emanate from the bottom-up as well as from the top down. The nature of the initiative focuses heavily on 'capturing knowledge': collecting knowledge on a world-wide scale and placing it in a database in order to make it accessible. The quality of the contents that is offered is therefore an important issue. A world-wide editorial team made up of experts evaluates the information before it is made available through ICM. The employees who have carried out a project for a client forward their information to this editorial team. It is their responsibility to keep the database up-to-date.

IBM Asset Web

The technical side of ICM is based on Lotus Notes. The IBM Asset Web (IBM-AW) was launched for this purpose, one with an intranet-comparable solution. The database offers access to all sorts of expertise and platforms. Tracking is carried out when IBM-AW is used. Apart from the technical performance, IBM has to ensure that using IBM-AW also offers advantages to the individual. Together with an award programme, this is also provided by the international recognition that an expert can amass. Such rewards stimulate colleagues who are not yet that far advanced.

Knowledge-sharing in practice

The implementation of ICM is based on an integrated approach. Eight points have to be in balance with one another: Vision, Strategy, Value, Processes, Organization, Technology, Incentives, and Measurements. ICM emerged following a major transformation to a service-driven organization. ICM is part of, and stimulates a change in, the teamwork culture. ICM's crystallization point is the IBM Asset Web, but at the same time a great deal of effort is being put into creating human networks. It touches all facets of the company. Apart from the recognition that ICM can offer a great deal to employees, the initiative also has to provide solid value to senior management. For example, it must be clear to both management and staff how many days are saved by recording and reusing knowledge.

Product and Support Services

In the Netherlands the introduction of ICM is highly advanced at Product and Support Services (PSS), which is part of Global Services. PSS has developed itself in the last few years from a 'maintenance' club to a supporter of innovations. Many of the people working at PSS have a technical background. These people do not see themselves as knowledge workers. They are individuals who are accustomed to an advanced level of automation. An important reason behind PSS becoming involved in ICM was that, on the one hand it wanted to deploy its personnel flexibly and, on the other hand, it wished to recycle knowledge wherever possible.

When it made the transition to a service-driven organization and world-wide collaboration, IBM showed that it managed knowledge inefficiently. IBM is continuously reinventing the wheel in some part of the world or another. This also has something to do with a curious cultural idiosyncrasy known as the 'not invented here' syndrome.

The manager of Product and Support Services considers the reuse of knowledge to be essential for his business:

'Knowledge is present throughout the world. The question is how you can use it. How do you stimulate giving and taking? A piece of personal knowledge management lies at the heart of this. In a technical environment people do not tend to jealously guard their knowledge. Technocrats feel more at ease perhaps about exchanging ideas. What is difficult is that people are not really prepared to start reusing knowledge. It is part of a technocrat's nature to want to invent something new rather than dig the solution out of the database'.

In order to stimulate knowledge reuse on an individual level, targets are set in the Personal Business Commitment. The ICM project group has promised even more rewards in this phase of 2500 to 5000 US dollars for major achievements in the area of contributing (or reusing) knowledge. The ICM project group further stimulates management in particular to give space and time to contribute to ICM.

PSS has a great need to reuse information for software development. There is both an internal motive as well as an external incentive for this. The growth in personnel cannot keep pace with the exponential growth of the company. In order to continue to help clients it is necessary to manage the available knowledge efficiently. Under the present circumstances, people tend to change jobs more quickly; IBM is therefore trying to retain at least some of this knowledge. PSS uses ICM for software development and when it prepares an estimate for a client. One of the people we interviewed told us:

'By taking a good look at what we have already done in-house, PSS can quickly produce an estimate. If you want to quickly build up a client relationship then you must recycle knowledge elements. Reusing software - isolating a code - is the key word with ICM.'.

Recycling requires a greater standardization of a customer's operations:

'You can offer standard solutions for a product such as Tivoli, but clients demand more efficiency on the one hand, while often insisting upon more than the standard solution on the other.'

Architects determine what is generic to a project and what lends itself well to reuse. PSS chose to record knowledge in a formal way. The database is the ideal tool to stimulate the reuse of knowledge. People are expected to make knowledge, offers and draft projects, available. In addition, there are also platforms where like-minded individuals throughout the world can exchange knowledge. A significant expansion has taken place in the form of electronic traffic and communication between people. This all has to do with connecting people. Extensive databases support this communication process.

5.2   Experiences

One of the major problems is that employees experience ICM as an extra activity. People are under great pressure with regard to time and often start to think ahead about new activities well before current projects are finished. They view writing down their impressions as an extra investment in time. The work pressure is extremely high.

Ideally, at the end of each project people should be given a couple of days to determine which knowledge is suitable for reuse. This space is often just not available. Managers from the ICM workgroup in particular are encouraged to give people the space to do this. Also, because of this, IBM considers it important to know what the excess value of ICM is, preferably in terms of increased profits or reduced costs. The ICM project is gearing itself up to demonstrate these excess values, as is evident in a report entitled 'How to make additional profit through IBM ICM.'

One practical problem is that people do not view their work as being to increase the 'intellectual capital' but simply as 'business as usual'. People cannot recognize what would be suitable for reuse from their work or sometimes even try to safeguard their intellectual capital. Knowledge-sharing requires constant management and encouragement from people. One of PSS's structural solutions was to allow architects to take part in the design phase of a project whereby they were able to contribute generic knowledge.

When ICM is used effectively a better-suited management style is one that focuses more on coaching than controlling. Management must be prepared to share knowledge. It is encouraging that in the nineties IBM ceased to be a 'white-collar company' and became instead a company with few hierarchical barriers. The culture at IBM is dominated by the term 'win-execute-team'. Team formation is important for performance. It is precisely this team-element that means that people must be prepared to both contribute and acquire knowledge. Working within a team also means that you are expected to share your training experiences during team meetings. People need incentives during this phase in the form of awards and the PBC. Furthermore, people who are not disposed to participating in this type of exercise or who prefer to treat their knowledge as a strategic commodity end up looking for a different work environment of their own volition.

It is clear to the ICM project group that all the components are important for ICM. A survey has revealed that 95 percent of the staff are aware of IBM-AW. Half of the employees are registered as users. The human factor - the creation of a basis for support and discipline - seems to be more important that a streamlined system. The ICM project group will consider its initiatives to be successful when it reaches the point at which it can demonstrate that it has outlived its usefulness. By then ICM should have become an integral part of the standard processes. Until that point, it is very important that it proves its worth. In England the necessary successes have already been accomplished. In addition, personal experiences, reactions and the first savings have also been demonstrated. More attention still has to be given, however, to demonstrating its value.

It is clear to PSS that ICM is valuable to the company. One of the people interviewed said:

'Even more importantly, if IBM did not pay any attention to ICM then profits would fall; IBM would end up serving the market too late. The margin would be lowered if IBM would not manage its resources efficiently.'

Although ICM's success has been proven, namely in England, different people involved complain that it is still being introduced too slowly. Since knowledge-sharing is so strongly related to the culture and because IBM is still in the midst of a transition phase, these initiatives are running parallel to one another.

Enablers
- support of senior management
- proven results
- simultaneous change in the culture
- temporary rewards
- integral changes
- client wants quicker solutions

Potential risks
- time pressures on the staff
- the system's technical performance
- slow cultural change
-   the compulsion to do things independently and develop them oneself

6. DISCUSSION: THE INDIVIDUAL AS KNOWLEDGE PROVIDER

Table 6 presents an overview of the characteristics of the knowledge-sharing process such as those that have been discussed in the case studies in this chapter.

Objective
It is hard to evaluate success at an individual or organizational level. Most companies do not have any formalized objectives with regard to knowledge-sharing. To use popular management jargon: there is often no 'business case' present. For managers it often only counts when knowledge-sharing can be made visible in solid performance norms - only then will they pay attention to it. One of the people interviewed, a general manager from one of the business units, said that for a long time he had had the same feeling about knowledge management as he did with the term quality:

'If no explicit standards exist, for example in the form of ISO-standards, then a manager cannot manage it and so you should not pay any attention to it.'

Table 6. Features of practical situations

Learning process	Schiphol	ING	Cap Gemini	IBM
Objective	To record personal knowledge and identify networks	To make country information available	To make knowledge accessible and to increase efficiency	To make knowledge accessible, to set standards, and to arrive at solutions more rapidly
ICT	Network	Intranet	Intranet	Intranet
Role of ICT	Limited	Important	Important	Important
Worker profile	Policy, knowledge work	Policy, knowledge work	Routine knowledge worker	Routine knowledge worker
Type of learning process	Capturing knowledge from, among others, personal networks	Making countries accessible	Reusing knowledge for the benefit of clients	Reusing knowledge for the benefit of clients
Support for the learning process	Knowledge Centre	Network of different countries	Informal networks and CapCom	Technical network
Experiences	Ensures cooperation	Scope too vast, problems with mobilization	Difference between bottom-up and top down initiative, time constraints	Forms part of the change process. Time and acknowledge-ment problem.

Now that there are tools available for this, the barrier for managers seems to have been removed. Other managers also warn about permanently setting down knowledge-sharing standards and writing down the benefits. It is also a concept which one must trust will contribute to the improved performance of the organization.

One of the most important objectives for the different companies involved in knowledge-sharing is the reuse of knowledge. Companies such as Cap Gemini say - certainly in the area of product development - that they are not able to be innovative because the market in which they operate does not allow for too much innovation. Clients prefer to have tested or reused solutions rather than solutions in which knowledge development virtually takes place during the execution of the project. The business model is geared towards being used again.

Both IBM Services and Cap Gemini are comparable with case studies that have been described elsewhere such as Ernst & Young and KPMG. These companies have opted to use their intellectual capital as effectively as possible, given certain market features or specific customer requirements. These companies operate in segments where added value is created by quickly making standard solutions specific to clients' needs (see also Hansen et al 1999). The so-called 'lock-in' arises here in which a client does not want any knowledge development within his or her project, but rather prefers to have a solution based on knowledge that has been tested somewhere else. In order to fulfil this requirement, companies have to push their employees to such an extent that they are prepared to make their own personal knowledge available and at the same time use their spare time to create knowledge with their colleagues.

Although there are obvious similarities between IBM and Cap Gemini - especially concerning the external pressure to begin reusing knowledge - there are also important differences. At Cap Gemini the first knowledge-sharing initiatives came mainly from the bottom-up within the organization. There was an in-house need at Cap Gemini to create networks and to make an intranet. In this respect, Cap Gemini chose a technical solution, which had insufficient support within the organization. There was no support for it either from the professionals or senior management. In addition to this, the solution chosen was an intranet with an excess of functions too complicated even for an ICT environment.

At IBM the initiative came from different quarters, but received direct and positive backing from the highest official. He used the ICM initiative within the framework of the global transformation that IBM is going through. Besides, it is not as if the whole of IBM is already contributing to the realization of ICM. The cultural changes that IBM thereby addresses, can contribute to the success of ICM, but even here it is uncertain whether the change will go ahead.

The big difference between Cap Gemini and IBM lies in the structure of the intranet. Cap Gemini opted for an anarchic structure with the features of a bottom-up initiative. In contrast to this, IBM chose for a structured approach. Those responsible for the initiative consider the support of senior management to be essential for knowledge management. Initiatives that stimulate knowledge-sharing but do not fit in with the needs of either the individual or the organization have a greater chance of failing. Even initiatives that come from the top have a weaker chance of success in a professional environment.

Intranets and knowledge exchange
For the organizations that came up for discussion in this chapter, disclosure via an intranet represents an important way of making knowledge accessible. The problems organizations encounter with the use of intranets include accessibility, keeping it up-to-date and having faith in technology as the solution. A danger attached to sharing

knowledge via the intranet is that the existence of an electronic network will reduce personal contacts. However, through formal knowledge exchange via an intranet and simultaneously stimulating knowledge exchange through informal channels too, companies increase their chances of strengthening the learning processes.

Among professional (knowledge)workers, knowledge acquisition from other individuals frequently takes place via personal contacts. It is through other colleagues that you will eventually find the person with the right expertise. Organizations have a tendency to formalize this knowledge flow via personal networks. This type of formalization can actually overreach its objective. For example, as soon as a colleague records his or her experiences in a document people are more inclined to contact the individual in person to exchange knowledge than simply consult the documents. Compared to Japanese companies, where usually great value is attached to people's tacit knowledge (Nonaka 1993), many western companies choose a codifying strategy and often introduce an intranet. The danger that belies the western perspective arises when organizations introduce a technical infrastructure that does not comply with the organization's work method, or when a technical replacement for a human interaction is sought.

Next to such a socio-technical approach to intranets, another requirement for the successful use and development of an intranet is the existence of a critical mass (Markus 1991). The more people contribute to the intranet, the more it will be used, and vice versa. This is often problematic because intranets are not always a very attractive medium to use. For example, they are complex with regard to their accessibility and often have outdated information. Moreover, there is a real danger of making too much information accessible. In short, a measured dose of up-to-date information that is both reliable and useful ensures that it is more likely to be used.

In order to have knowledge stored in an intranet considered reliable and useful it helps to select and filter information. This can be supported by an editorial board, experts or a jury who determine what should be made available, as was the case at IBM. At IBM, an editorial board with senior staff members decided which knowledge elements should form part of the electronic knowledge network. This increases the quality of the knowledge offered.

Intranets are often viewed as a source of information and not as a way of connecting people to one another. The organizational context and the importance of getting to know the people behind the knowledge are features that should be borne in mind. A very real dilemma is that it is hard to mobilize people and achieve a critical mass in organizations that have a wide geographical distribution as was the case at ING Barings bank. Yet it is these organizations that have the greatest need for it. In part three of the book, these and other aspects of codified knowledge and ICT use are discussed more intensively.

In chapter 9, we will discuss the use of intranets in supporting knowledge-sharing in more detail.

Knowledge work
The nature of the work at the companies presented in this chapter differs from the routine type of work that we discussed in the last chapter. The staff members, software developers, consultants and knowledge coordinators are all knowledge workers here. These people do not only process information but transform the information into knowledge.

Companies such as IBM and Cap Gemini are considering whether to reward individuals for contributing to the knowledge-sharing process when evaluating their performance. Tangible experiences with rewarding knowledge-sharing are still not actually available. Generally speaking, financial rewards only have a short-term effect. Incentives and rewards should be finely tuned with one another (Drew 1999). Companies can reward their employees with money, but also by allowing them to participate in more prestigious projects, or by giving them a special status.

ICT-service providers such as Cap Gemini and IBM witness a high level of mobility among people who are employed in this field. Moreover, they have to keep up-to-date in their sector and areas of technology. ICT-service providers are knowledge-driven enterprises where knowledge creation and knowledge reuse has an important place. It is precisely the business model of many service providers - whereby there is talk of maximizing the number of invoiced hours per person - that forces knowledge to be reused. Many organizations are faced with such a dilemma. Focussed initiatives are required in order to derive the optimum profits from the brainpower within the organizations, but measures from senior management are met with resistance from the professionals. ICT companies thereby choose the first step to codify the knowledge and to make it available through an intranet. In addition they transfer knowledge within the personal networks. People acquire knowledge within a network, sometimes standardized in an SIG or in a knowledge centre. In this sense, the personal network and the technological network go hand in hand. The combination of networks provided knowledge intensive companies with a foundation but also contained an inherent risk: personal networks often depend on people who, given the high degree of mobility, may leave the network. The knowledge on the intranet appears to be a poor substitute for this. Certainly among ICT-service providers such as IBM and Cap Gemini sometimes too great a level of optimism prevails about the value of codifying knowledge. Trust plays a central role in these networks; regardless of whether they have been technologically or organizationally supported. The power of personal networks is that people have faith in the reciprocal nature of the relationship (e.g. Fukuyama 1995, Gambetta 1988, Goshal and Nahapiet 1998).

Learning through knowledge exchange
Although different companies consider themselves knowledge intensive organizations and their employees 'knowledge workers', they often treat their employees more like knowledge tools than knowledge professionals. They choose to focus on codifying knowledge instead of exchanging knowledge, or only see a

possibility to profit as a company through externalizing knowledge. When we analyse this against a background of organizational learning processes we also see that organizations only have a limited degree of success in learning from knowledge reuse in their capacity as an organization.

We wanted to highlight a specific type of knowledge-sharing: that of making the individual's knowledge accessible to the organization. The four organizations aim to reuse knowledge. Reuse requires not only the individuals to learn within the company but also the organization to learn as a collective. At Schiphol Airport, ING Barings, Cap Gemini and IBM an explicit objective is indeed to make the knowledge of individuals accessible through knowledge centres, intranet and the SIGs. In figure 7 we have placed the different organizations next to the different types of learning.

IBM is the only company to have invented a structure for knowledge reuse to transform the contributed knowledge into organizational knowledge. This type of collective acceptance of knowledge does not occur at the other organizations. It is because IBM tries to objectify knowledge in a concrete way that we recognize different types of learning in this process. The organization learns from the experiences of individuals, who share their knowledge via communities on the intranet, whereby an editorial board oversees the value of the knowledge for the organization.

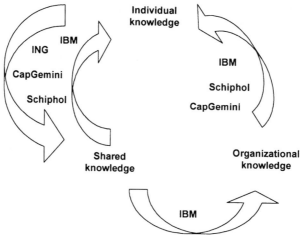

Figure 7. Organizations divided up according to learning processes.

At companies whose thinking is dominated by the 'not invented here' syndrome or by individual solutions, stimulating knowledge reuse has little effect if the change in culture is not focussed upon at the same time. This is also the lesson that IBM learned.

Cap Gemini occupies a special position. Even though no structure exists to ensure that the knowledge shared through personal or technical networks is collectively accepted, feedback is still given to the individual. In this instance, it concerns on the one hand routine knowledge such as templates and manuals, and on the other hand knowledge flowing through the informal networks. 'Best practices' are in the form of a collection of experiences and do not appear to have been carefully edited. At Cap Gemini knowledge-sharing and learning takes place primarily through personal networks.

Cap Gemini also illustrates an interesting dilemma. The first knowledge management initiatives originated from the middle management level within the organization, but were not very successful due to scant support from senior management. Because explicit knowledge objectives were put forward, the initiative that subsequently came from the top met with a great deal of resistance. This type of initiative does not fit in well with the existing culture in the company.

7. SUMMARY

This chapter focussed on the exchange of knowledge between individuals. The knowledge reuse practices of four different organizations were discussed: Schiphol Airport, ING Barings, Cap Gemini and IBM. We observed that these organizations try to use individuals' knowledge in as efficient a manner as possible. To do this they encourage employees to make their knowledge available to others. The four companies discussed in this chapter use technical and organizational networks to support this. They busy themselves with the question of how they can manage the knowledge of all the different individuals. The key question is: by what means can you enable the organization to benefit from the knowledge spread around within the organization? Most often, intranets are seen as the solution to this question.

CHAPTER 6

KNOWLEDGE DEVELOPMENT

Communities as knowledge providers

1. INTRODUCTION

In this chapter three case studies are discussed that are concerned with knowledge-sharing within 'communities'. The case studies originate from Stork, Unilever and the Ministry of Housing, Spatial Planning and the Environment in the Netherlands (Ministry of Housing). In different ways and for various reasons the organizations show how knowledge-sharing takes place within communities to bring about knowledge development and how this can be structured.

This chapter differs on two counts from the previous chapters. Firstly, in this chapter we approach learning not primarily as a way to reuse existing knowledge but rather as a method to develop new knowledge. In the previous chapter we discussed knowledge-sharing that was geared towards exchanging knowledge. Although in this chapter the emphasis is also on exchange or externalization, the primary objective is different. Knowledge exchange here is not aimed at diffusion and reuse, but rather at developing new knowledge. In the case studies on structured knowledge-sharing that are presented here, reusing existing knowledge is still an important motive, just as it was in the previous case studies. The difference is that the objective of this form of reuse is to create new combinations out of existing knowledge, comparable with Schumpeter's (1934) ideas on innovation.

Secondly, this chapter differs from the previous chapters because knowledge-sharing here is all about a reciprocal learning process. Up until now we have looked upon knowledge-sharing specifically as a one-sided learning process. In Chapter 4 we examined how individuals internalized organizational knowledge and the way in which companies can facilitate this process. In Chapter 5 knowledge-sharing processes were discussed in which it was mainly a matter of an exchange: individuals learning from other individuals within the organization. In both chapters learning was a way of using organizational and individual knowledge respectively. In this chapter we give examples of knowledge-sharing in which the accent is not so much on the knowledge-sharing between individuals but rather one level higher, at the group level or - in this case - the community level.

2. COMMUNITIES AS PLATFORMS FOR KNOWLEDGE DEVELOPMENT

First and foremost we will pause at the term 'communities' given that this represents the key concept for this chapter. In the next paragraph an example is given of how communities are used at Shell and how this is facilitated by different ICT-applications.

One viewpoint that perceives knowledge-sharing as a *collective* process rather than a sum total of individual processes, presents a different picture of the support for knowledge-sharing than has been discussed hitherto. This perspective uses so-called 'communities' as the unit of analysis (e.g. Brown and Duguid 1991, Lave and Wenger 1991, McDermott 1999, Wenger 1998). A community is based on shared activities and a shared need for knowledge (Starr 1992). When shared practices are stressed, most authors refer to 'Communities of Practice'.

The concept of communities of practice (COP) stems from learning theories not business theories and in specific studies of apprenticeship (Lave and Wenger 1991). The term community was coined to refer to the community that acts as a living curriculum for the apprentice. Then researchers started to see these communities everywhere, even when no formal apprenticeship system existed. The concept was quickly adopted in the field of business predominantly because of the positive connotation the word 'community' offers. It inspires people to think about alternative ways of organizing that depart from the rigid, impersonal, hierarchical way of organizing. It is extremely hard to find opponents to the concept. Had Lave and Wenger coined it differently, say as 'informal social networks', then the whole concept would probably not have taken off so quickly and with so much enthusiasm.

Communities
Communities are something other than the teams and other collective groupings referred to in most corporate literature (Table 7). Teams are accepted and structured entities while this is not necessarily the case with communities. In addition, the composition of communities can change, while the composition of teams is often fixed. Studies of the daily work practices of, among others, system analysts (Ciborra and Lanzara 1994), maintenance engineers (Orr 1990), midwives (Jordan 1989), flight crews and ground staff (Weick and Roberts 1993), indicate that within such communities collaborative forms of working and learning coincide with each other. From this perspective collective learning is an unavoidable aspect of participating in community life.

Table 7. Some characteristics of communities in comparison to teams (McDermott 1999)

Teams	Communities
Driven by deliverables	Driven by value
Shared goals and results	Shared interest or practice
Value defined	Value discovered/evolved
Value in result delivered	Value in ongoing process
Defined by task	Defined by knowledge
Interdependent tasks	Interdependent knowledge
Clear boundaries	Permeable boundaries
Develops through a workplan	Develops organically
Everyone contributes	Variable contributions
Managed through objectives and workplan	Managed by making decisions

The collective learning processes of communities are hard to manage as they are unpredictable bottom-up processes that exist in a situational context. The result of the collective learning processes within communities is 'situated knowledge'; knowledge that is not so much contained in systems or people's heads but in situations and activities (Lave and Wenger 1991). This is also the reason why it is difficult to establish communities from the top down. Snyder and Wenger (1999) talk about the 'management paradox'; the moment we want to manage these communities we will destroy their voluntary and specific nature. Case studies show that management has little influence over these communities and can do little more than recognize and accept them as they are (Brown and Duguid 1991).

Downsides of Communities of Practice
Communities of practice risk being viewed as very positive. But they have many downsides and these are important to note. For example, it is not difficult to think of examples of communities that are good at working, learning and organizing, but have negative consequences for their surroundings. Also, being part of a fixed community is not always as positive and romantic as outsiders might think it is. Imagine for example living in highly community-based villages. Thirdly, communities have their own 'signature skills' (Leonard 1995) which can be extremely difficult to change. They have the tendency to continue doing and thinking what they always did and thought, increasingly excluding outsiders, and becoming more and more conservative. Another downside of the concept is that the word itself 'community', connotes cooperation where there is no room for 'competition'. But community without friendly competition loses its edge (Brown and Duguid 2000). People take their learning and use of knowledge most seriously when they sense some competition (Nonaka 1995). When organizations strive for development and innovation, it

is important to recognize that communities can provide a feeling of belonging at the same time as a feeling of competing. Similarly, the word 'communities' connotes democracy and equality while some form of hierarchy seems to be needed to stay connected with the environment (Huysman and Van Baalen, 2002). Finally, the concept itself runs the risk of being used as a container concept. Because of its romantic connotation, it has inspired many organizational theorists and practitioners to label social groups ranging from business teams to friendship networks as being communities.

To avoid this danger of being used as a container concept, Wenger (1999) distinguish three characteristics of Communities of practice that are crucial and which distinguish them from other communities like neighbourhoods:

The domain:
Membership implies a minimum level of knowledge of that domain (e.g. tomato sauce production at Unilever). It refers to a shared competence that distinguishes members from other people. While informal networks are based on informal relationships, communities of practice are based on domains.

The community
Members interact and learn to pursue their collective interest in the domain, for example by engaging in joint activities and discussions, helping each other and sharing information.

The practice
Members share a repertoire of resources: experiences, stories, tools, ways of addressing recurring problems: a shared practice. Shared meaning is certainly not the reason to flock together, it is the practice that brings people together.

Communities at Shell

Shell has had several years' experience with 'communities of interest networks'. Shell also has a lot of networks, mainly as a result of the large number of experts and the importance of the training centre where experts meet every year. The first communities began on the shop floor. However, subsequent initiatives came from a unit within Shell called 'New Ways of Working' that had an advisory role.

One of the successful examples is Shell's OGHB instrumentation-team. The number of engineers on this team dropped from seventy to twelve due to automation. The staff had to develop themselves more on a broad-range level than on an in-depth level, but they also needed each other's expertise more. Communication within this community began with e-mail, followed by a news forum, a knowledge database and a website. The knowledge database contains, among other things, 'best practices'.

The communities at Shell have a 'moderator' who has to spend about 20 percent of her time on keeping a community going. This moderator fulfils different roles and must be highly motivated. A moderator contributes to the culture of a community by maintaining a specific language style, editing texts, or reformulating questions. She is both architect and editor at the same time. Only the moderator can decide whether documents or links may be added to the knowledge database.

Shell maintains that it has had visible, positive experiences with this type of knowledge-sharing. For every hour spent, Shell gets seven back. There are examples of countries that have copied operational instructions or designs. The estimated profit in time saved works out at 15 million US dollars.

2.1   The technology

Communities are supported in many different ways. Shell, for example, uses intranet-technology. With regard to supporting (synchronous) communication there are also video-conferencing systems or e-mail, news groups, discussion groups or simply the telephone. Interaction on an intranet occurs asynchronously in many cases, although this type of network usually also offers a 'chat' facility. Different kinds of ICT support are often required to facilitate knowledge development where employees create new knowledge by interacting with one another (Blackler 1995). Examples of this are Computer Supported Cooperative Work systems (CSCW) which can be divided into two categories:

- *asynchronous systems.* These systems offer support to people who are not working on the same task simultaneously, such as e-mail, news groups, mailing lists, workflow systems, certain document systems and hypertext. We see these systems being used particularly for knowledge gathering and knowledge exchange too.

- *Synchronous systems.* The systems offer support to people who are working on the same task simultaneously in real time. This relates to different conference systems (video, audio). In addition, this category includes advanced applications such as group-decision support systems, virtual space and shared white boards.

These applications facilitate key operations within organizations such as communication and teamwork. Knowledge is often shared knowledge, part of the corporate culture and is understood collectively. People are geared towards developing new knowledge, dialogue and 'making sense'. We can recognize this type of organization in R&D environments and advertising agencies. A number of R&D environments are discussed in this chapter too. The level of acceptance for ICT varied from 'accepted' to 'not installed'. For example, Stork still just uses diskettes as the only ICT based medium to support knowledge-sharing in communities. Unilever has installed intranet-technology in order to support asynchronous communication and uses software tools to record knowledge. The Ministry of Housing mainly uses the Internet for its external communications.

Knowledge development in practice

In the rest of this chapter we discuss the experiences of Stork, Unilever and the Ministry of Housing as examples of structured forms of knowledge development within communities.

In this context, Stork has the tradition of the 'integrated process innovation' (IPI). This structure supports different communities enabling them to share knowledge and allow new knowledge to come into existence. Unilever organizes 'knowledge workshops' to exchange and create new knowledge. As a result of these workshops, communities emerge that might guarantee knowledge development in the future. The Ministry has 'electronic communities'. It uses the Internet so that communities focussing on a specific theme can exchange thoughts. The Ministry also incorporates the results of this type of electronic discussion platform in its future policy development.

3. KNOWLEDGE DEVELOPMENT VIA WORKING GROUPS AT STORK

A description of knowledge development at Stork offers an insight into the way in which knowledge creation is facilitated within social networks. ICT does not play any meaningful role with regard to supporting this form of knowledge development. Nevertheless, we decided to use this case as an illustration, mainly because of the innovative way in which Stork has structured knowledge development. What makes this case especially interesting is the fact that the communities have existed for more than 25 years already and are still supported by senior management.

The working group structure is called Integrated Process Innovation (IPI). The aim of IPI is to improve the primary operations and support processes at the different subsidiaries. IPI has recently been dubbed with the label 'knowledge management'.

> **Profile of Stork**
> Stork is a technology company with operations world-wide. Its clients are generally speaking either producers or users of production systems or technological services. Stork employs some twenty thousand people and they produce a turnover of two billion US dollars. Stork has chosen for a highly decentralized type of organization. It now has eighty-five subsidiary companies operating under it and these have been divided over five groups: Textile Printing, Food Processing, Aerospace, Technical Services, and Engineering. Stork's most important markets are the processing and aerospace industries.

The eighty-five subsidiary companies are responsible for their own profits. Stork's decentralized design enables it to operate in close proximity with its clients. Moreover, employees can identify more closely with the branch of the company which makes them more motivated. The decentralized nature of Stork was established in the 1970s when the company was split up into more financially digestible units. One of the characteristics of Stork is the fact that its products have very little in common with each other. Stork recognizes this weakness: achieving synergy is therefore an important theme.

The directors of the subsidiary companies have a lot of freedom to take care of their business themselves, as long as they can show a profit. Stork aims to strengthen core competences. It recognizes them in particular in 'the development, design and production of appliances, components and systems and the provision of multidisciplinary services to industrial clients.

3.1   The knowledge initiative

Knowledge intensity is a strategic issue for Stork. In order to tap into basic knowledge, Stork works together with large technology institutes and technical universities. Technology is of vital importance for a company operating in an industrial environment. In every branch of the market Stork translates basic technological knowledge into applications. This requires knowledge of both the market branch and the technology. There are also different initiatives that can be grouped under the common term 'knowledge management'. One recent initiative concentrates on establishing so-called 'centres of excellence' that focus on awareness and exploration of new themes such as ERP-software and Total Quality Management.

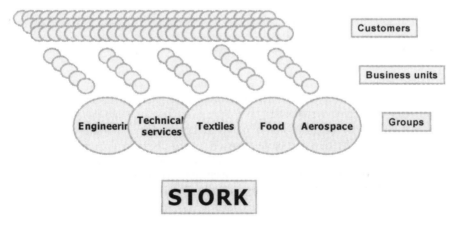

Figure 8. Stork's organizational structure

Subsidiary companies have their own projects, for example to initiate product development and stimulate a better understanding of clients. Important initiatives have been taken on a subsidiary level to stimulate the transfer of knowledge from the outside to the inside (from the knowledge infrastructure to Stork or to increase knowledge about the clients). Although the term knowledge management has now become quite popular, Stork prefers to refer to it as 'using knowledge to assist our customers'.

As a decentrally organized enterprise, Stork needs to boost knowledge synergy. This takes place by connecting the knowledge centres of the subsidiary companies to about four knowledge networks. The knowledge networks transcend the boundaries of the separate subsidiaries. The knowledge centres come up with research programmes that Stork subsequently outsources to the universities and applied research institutes. This is how Stork manages to accomplish the transfer of knowledge from outside the company to the inside.

Eighteen knowledge clusters exist within the knowledge networks in which specialists from the different subsidiary companies participate. The knowledge exchange process focuses on developing new knowledge and sharing knowledge between people in different subsidiaries. One of the tools used for this is Integrated Process Innovation (IPI): the working group structure that transcends the subsidiary company.

The structure of knowledge-sharing
IPI's mission is to stimulate and coordinate new developments for Stork companies and to make improvements to the company's key operations. IPI attempts to make the maximum use of the potential for synergy by creating personal and external networks through which the available knowledge is increased and made accessible to Stork companies. IPI stands for synergy and knowledge management. Knowledge here refers to expert knowledge: knowledge of the markets, customer operations and one's own in-house operations. IPI stimulates the development of this type of knowledge.

At the beginning of the 1970s Stork's traditional activities were split. Up until that point Stork's product package consisted of capital goods such as pumps, filing systems and packaging systems and textile printing. Research and development took place, among others, at the subsidiary company Physical Dynamic Research (FDO). During the reorganization the large divisions were chopped up into subsidiaries. FDO's place was discussed within this structure. At the subsidiary companies knowledge was mainly present in the form of product knowledge or knowledge of the local production process. Soon, the different companies developed the need for activities that transcended the subsidiary level.

IPI is based on a 1970s initiative when a number of technological working groups were launched. Numerical control was one of the first subjects to be discussed here.

The idea was to share experiences within a working group to avoid a situation in which every company would end up reinventing the wheel. The initiative clearly came from the bottom-up. When the initiative was expanded it was given more structure. Roundabout 1980 IPI changed over from being function-driven and became operation-driven. Over the years, more and more production operations and management processes have been studied.

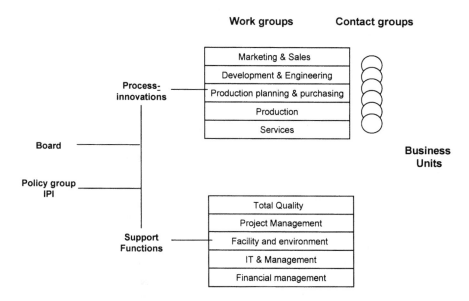

Figure 9. IPI's working groups structure

IPI has two steering groups: a steering group called Process Innovation and a steering group called Support Functions. Working groups on Marketing and Sales, Development and Engineering, Process Planning and Purchasing, and Production and Service, come under the umbrella of the Process Innovation steering group. The working groups on Total Quality, Project Management, Environment and Facility Management, Financial and Economic Management, and IT and Management belong to the Support Functions steering group. The working groups can establish contact groups that bring professional experts from a specific subject area together and can also initiate projects (see figure 9).

The working groups have a facilitator whose task is to organize and initiate activities. The facilitators are in charge of a specific subject area: they stimulate interest in new developments, draw attention to new developments, represent Stork externally and link up the working groups to national and international projects. Their task is to make sure that the working group remains active and dynamic. They spring into action if the working groups become too small or too inward looking. The facilitators are experienced people within Stork with extensive personal networks. Their charisma and seniority also determines to a certain degree IPI's success. It is important for the facilitators to have a Chair who is expert in a specific field. Chairs must have a broad vision concerning certain areas of expertise.

3.2 Experiences

IPI has gone through an internal transformation. In the beginning it was something of an elite club primarily consisting of experts from specific fields. The results of the working groups were hardly ever put to use. One of the people we interviewed remembered it like this:

> 'They were the smart guys with the lengthy reports, but that was just the way things were then'.

Later on there was a phase in which many management issues were discussed, but here again insufficient attention was given to innovations in the area of company operations. These days it seems that the balance has been regained.

The main form of knowledge exchange occurs within the working groups as they are active in different subject areas. Between ten to fifteen subsidiaries from the various Stork companies participate in the working groups. The working groups play an innovative role and act as networks. They do this by contributing expert knowledge. Working groups have different tasks:
− to monitor the broad area in which results can be applied;
− to establish a basis for change;
− to encourage the acceptance of proposals; and,
− to bring about the dissemination of results.
People either sign up for the working groups or are invited to join. Employees often become long-standing members of a working group. Project groups are transient by nature. They also consist of outside bodies, such as technical universities. Projects have various forms of teamwork and various forms of financing. A total of between 300 to 400 people are involved in IPI.

There is an inherent sluggishness in IPI's structure due to the nature of the working groups and the project groups. As one of the interviewees put it:

> 'IPI is not short of ideas, nor does it want for funding, but it does lack tempo.'

The procedures to set up a working group or a theme take up a lot of time. Consequently, when quick results are needed for an up-to-the-minute theme Stork employs a separate structure in the form of projects.

The working groups still do not receive any direct support with the help of information technology, although last year a rudimentary form of ICT was used. With this, 150 reports were placed on a diskette and disseminated within Stork. The company is now engaged in building an intranet and it is expected that this will enable IPI's results to be disseminated more effectively and rapidly.

The members of the working groups are, generally speaking, quite active and are usually prominent employees at Stork. The members participate in the working group as part of their daily work. They receive recognition and respect for this. They are allowed to participate in the projects as long as this does not impede their other work. Those involved have been members of the working group for years. On average, participation in the working group takes up twelve days of every year. However, the participants often remain involved in the activities even when they are no longer members of the working group. This is how informal networks are created.

IPI stimulates innovation within Stork by initiating projects and setting aside budgets for them. Projects can only take off if the initiative has the support of at least four subsidiaries. Knowledge that has been gathered during a project must remain anchored and accessible within Stork. By organizing theme days, the working groups can ensure that their project results are disseminated and so each working group is invited to organize one theme day a year.

Through IPI, Stork has learned to avoid the 'ivory-tower' mentality and to generate sufficient support at its subsidiaries. Examples of projects that have had a great impact are the 'three factories'-design, professional subcontracting, and benchmarking. Knowledge institutes or advice agencies are regularly involved when a project is implemented.

People often participate in knowledge management on a voluntary basis. Stork's decentralized structure forces people to justify their participation in working groups to their immediate superior and to demonstrate its usefulness. The voluntary aspect is one of the most difficult issues mainly because people take part alongside their operational duties. This means, in general, that participants can only be present at three out of four meetings. Recently, in order to increase IPI's foothold within the organization, it was decided to elevate and expand the working groups' membership base by deliberately inviting the managers and directors to join. However, one disadvantage is that directors usually have difficulty in abandoning their primary tasks.

IPI is a method of achieving synergy and coherence. Yet this structured type of knowledge development is less successful than we might imagine, given its length of existence. Some Stork employees are dubious about the results of the knowledge development that takes place between the members of the different working groups. This is because a great deal of the acquired knowledge is put into reports that simply end up in the drawer. Important reasons for this can be found in the organization's decentralized structure and culture. Another problem for IPI is that, because of its mission, it has to look way beyond a two-year term, while subsidiaries prefer to see quicker results. What is striking is that most of Stork's profit-making companies make greater use of IPI than the less profitable ones. Companies such as Stork PMT joined in enthusiastically with the pilot studies, not only because they liked to be trend-setters within Stork, but also in order to learn from the pilot studies conducted in their own company.

Despite the fact that Stork employees only occasionally use the results of knowledge-sharing at a later stage, the IPI structure can still survive for decades. Different explanations can be given for this. One explanation can be found in the enthusiasm with which the two facilitators initiate and support the activities of the different working groups. These two inspiring individuals work full-time at maintaining the structure. They do this by approaching people to take part in the working groups, inviting guests, placing new topics on the agenda and arranging meetings for the working groups. The seniority and social skills of both these charismatic individuals are also an important stimulus here. Secondly, the working groups remain active because their members enjoy participating in a network that spans the entire organization. People take part in the working groups on a voluntary basis and members view them as an opportunity to network informally and to lobby.

It is hard to measure the impact of IPI, yet it costs half a million US dollars per year. It is one of the few structured means that Stork has at its disposal to stimulate knowledge exchange between the business segments. However, it is clear that reports alone are not enough.

Enablers
- support from senior management
- seniority of those taking the initiative
- networking opportunities for the participants
- support from the subsidiaries
- established structure

Potential risks
- insufficient reconciliation with what is needed
- image of an 'ivory-tower' club
- limited use of knowledge
- decentralized aspect of Stork organization

4. KNOWLEDGE DEVELOPMENT VIA WORKSHOPS AT UNILEVER RESEARCH[7]

One of the most important knowledge initiatives at Unilever is the Culinary Knowledge Initiative. Culinary is a product category that was created in 1995 with an important footing in tomato-based products. The aim of Culinary is to become one of the key-players in its product area. An innovative and expansive strategy has been formulated to achieve this. Capitalizing on knowledge is an important way of implementing that strategy.

There was a need within the tomato product-processing sector to obtain insights into the accessible knowledge and the knowledge gaps in the supply chain of tomato products. This is because different companies that were scattered over a wide geographical area had been taken over within a very short time. In many of these factories similar products were being created in totally different ways. The question was whether the differences could be explained. Traditionally, when such a question is posed, a knowledge engineer would travel around the world, map out the knowledge of different experts and, on the basis of this, would identify the knowledge gaps. This method of working really takes up a lot of time and generates a substantial amount of feedback. A method was therefore needed to make knowledge mapping an easier process. The initiative for a knowledge workshop originated from this need.

Profile of Unilever
Unilever is a multinational company specializing in consumer products in the areas of food, cosmetics and detergents. The company has more than 90 branches world-wide and a turnover of roughly 35 billion dollars. Investment in research and product development amounted to .7 billion dollars in 1998.

Unilever is a company with a highly decentralized organizational structure. Corporate decisions are taken mainly in London and Rotterdam, while the factories are responsible for operations.

Unilever feels driven to shorten the innovation cycle of its consumer products. For several years Unilever Research focussed on knowledge management as one of the ways to enable people within the organization to exchange knowledge quickly.

The start of the knowledge workshops was a coincidence. An expert meeting that had already been scheduled in Bangalore (India) to deal with a specific problem when producing ketchup was requisitioned at the time to hold the first knowledge workshop. After this first session different workshops were held within Culinary. The first step was to trace what knowledge there was and what knowledge was missing concerning the production of tomato-based products. Fifty critical issues were identified during the first sessions.

Unilever later went on to develop the methodology for the workshops as part of the SHARK-project. This acronym stands for Sharing and Reuse of Knowledge. The objective behind recording the knowledge gaps is ultimately to produce innovations in products or improvements in the operational process, in this instance the Culinary Knowledge Initiative.

So far 25 workshops have taken place, the majority of which were in the Culinary division. Approximately 250 people have participated in the knowledge workshops. The workshops ultimately produced three different results:
- a community of practice;
- a Tomato-Knowledge system based on Lotus Notes;
- an overview of knowledge gaps in project descriptions.

Traditionally, a new product was considered the most important result of an innovation process. The Culinary Knowledge Initiative led to the point where knowledge in itself was an important result. The initiative contains additional regular evaluations about knowledge construction in projects. Evaluations are held both during a project and once it has been completed. In this way project teams begin to view knowledge as a supplementary result.

4.1   The knowledge initiative

For several decades now senior management has been emphasizing the importance of knowledge for Unilever. Knowledge and knowledge exchange ultimately determines Unilever's success in the marketplace. Unilever considers it its mission to use its knowledge and international experience to serve its local clients. For this purpose Unilever envisages different knowledge exchange processes: internal knowledge exchange between specialists, the transfer of knowledge from universities to Unilever, the transfer of internal knowledge to the client and learning from intensive knowledge about consumers.

The initial steps toward the systematic collection, creation, and exchange of knowledge and the concern for an organizational memory began five years ago during a strategic planning meeting. Unilever competed more fiercely with prices and watched its innovative products being replicated too quickly by its competitors. As a consequence, Unilever felt obliged to reduce the innovation cycle of its consumer products. Knowledge played an important role in this. In order to use existing knowledge within the organization more efficiently, knowledge exchange and development has become a central issue.

Unilever recognizes three pillars to its knowledge-sharing, as illustrated in Figure 10: knowledge processes, technological support and tuning in with the organization. In addition, it attaches a lot of importance to the human factor and to subtle incentives. As a rule of thumb, Unilever uses a 20-30-50 model:
- 20 percent of the attention goes on technology (Technical problems can be solved relatively easily)
- 30 percent of the attention goes on knowledge processes.
- 50 percent of the attention goes to the corporate, human and cultural aspects.

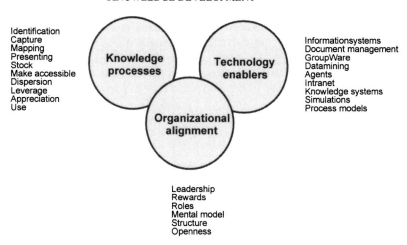

Identification
Capture
Mapping
Presenting
Stock
Make accessible
Dispersion
Leverage
Appreciation
Use

Informationsystems
Document management
GroupWare
Datamining
Agents
Intranet
Knowledge systems
Simulations
Process models

Leadership
Rewards
Roles
Mental model
Structure
Openness

Figure 10. Conceptual design of knowledge management at Unilever

Unilever's communities involve social networks of individuals scattered over a wide geographical area. Individuals find each other through a commonly shared need for knowledge. When they meet in person knowledge exchange takes place and new knowledge is created on the spot. What is interesting is that these communities stem from individual interest, though they exist through the intervention of management.

Although Unilever has been occupied with knowledge exchange for a while it tries to avoid the term knowledge management as often as possible. This is because they associate the term with domination and control and feel that it takes away the significance of the human factor in knowledge exchange.

4.2   Experiences

Unilever's initiatives in the area of knowledge management cover not only the strategic level but also the operational level. Drawing up plans to support company strategy through knowledge development and knowledge exchange occurs on a strategic level. Factual knowledge exchange comes into its own on an operational level.

Up to now the Knowledge Mapping and Structuring department of Unilever Research has organized the knowledge workshops. The term 'Knowledge Mapping and Structuring' has its origins in the world of knowledge technology. The employees who are involved in this have a background in knowledge technology and are also knowledgeable about technical fields that are relevant to Unilever. Holding workshops turned out to be a successful way of stimulating exchange processes. Unilever values the knowledge workshops highly because they represent a means to bring people together and to encourage exchange.

Three people lead knowledge workshops: a facilitator, a co-facilitator and a chair. The chair and co-facilitator must be knowledgeable about the subject area. The facilitator must be familiar with the subject but, in particular, he or she should know all about knowledge engineering and how to facilitate groups. The latter also applies to the co-facilitator. The facilitator should know how to present the right knowledge questions in order to keep the group on its toes. The workshops stick to a fixed pattern. The knowledge workshop consists of knowledge sessions (plenary and in sub-groups) in which people create a knowledge map based on a knowledge framework. In this situation it is important to speak a common language. The knowledge framework is the communication tool. Both the existing knowledge and how the knowledge can be linked up are mapped out based on products, product brands, operations and ingredients. In addition, the facilitator makes use of group facilitating techniques and interactive tools. At the same time graphic and text overheads of knowledge are projected to facilitate continuous validation.

It is the facilitator's task to maintain the balance of the group. By stressing the social side of the knowledge workshops they provide an opportunity for trust to be established between the participants and to highlight its special attributes. Most of the workshops take place in exotic locations outside the usual workplace; a feature that certainly boosts members' identification with the group.

At the beginning of the workshop people are praised for their attendance. Often the senior executive will go on to stress the importance of this type of activity for Unilever. The knowledge workshops focus a lot of attention on building up trusting relationships between the different experts. During the preparations for the workshop as well as the first sessions a lot of attention is given to creating a shared language and frame of reference to quickly establish a feeling of belonging to the group among members.

Generally speaking, the people who take part in the knowledge workshops have been employed at Unilever for a long time. Participants are also often experts in a specific area while the invited guests tend to be people with a passion for the subject area. Discussions about the theme simply continue through the night in the bar. This commonly shared passion makes it easy to overcome any cultural differences that might arise.

Knowledge workshops bring specialists together to focus on a specific subject area. So far that area has always reflected one activity within Unilever but there are now attempts to unite the different disciplines, such as technology, maintenance, quality control, product development and processing. A combination of empirical knowledge and theoretical knowledge is often present.

The most important result of the knowledge workshop is the ability to identify what Unilever does know and what it does not know about a specific product. The effect of the workshops goes beyond identifying knowledge gaps. During the process of identifying knowledge while interacting in the workshop, new knowledge is created. It can therefore be said that sharing knowledge leads to new insights.

The tomato workshops had a lot of short-term effects. For example, participants realized that the problems they were encountering locally had been largely solved elsewhere within Unilever. This contributed to individual learning at Unilever. What began as an operation for Unilever turned out to have a substantial impact at the individual level.

The knowledge workshops progressed as communities. It took between nine months to one year to mould these networks. Communities need a sponsor and are at their most effective when they focus on a specific subject area. Unilever considers its knowledge management initiatives to be of strategic value, producing both short term and long term results. The knowledge workshops have increasingly become a means to stimulate knowledge creation and knowledge exchange. One attractive example is that when a new factory for tomato products was being developed the knowledge of a community was used which enabled the factory to be realized much more quickly. Indeed, participants find it stimulating when they see people being drawn into strategic projects after they have participated in a knowledge workshop. It remains difficult to record the results of knowledge workshops in financial terms.

Knowledge workshops are now also being established in other subject disciplines. The methodology can obviously be passed on, however enthusiasm and effort is needed to generate involvement at the different levels. There are people at the highest level within Unilever who believe in these ideas and who know how to generate involvement as sponsors. Subsidiaries must be able to recognize the value of knowledge workshops. This is needed because, in order to participate, people have to be withdrawn from operational activities for two weeks. Unilever's recognition of someone's individual expertise through his or her contribution to the international network can differ greatly from how it is appreciated at the local level and this can be a source of conflict. This source of conflict will increase as Unilever companies begin working more closely with each other due to globalization.

One specific problem for Unilever is that factories in different countries can be each others' competitors. It is therefore difficult for some people to work together in a workshop and be completely open about their knowledge. This is discussed in depth beforehand with the participants. Another problem is that ultimately too little happens with the workshop's results. There is seldom even a follow-up to the workshop. The momentum of the workshop is not maintained. This is because the database is no longer consulted once the knowledge has been identified and the knowledge gaps recorded.

ICT is not an important focal point in the knowledge initiative. While it is true that technology is used during the knowledge capturing process, nevertheless no official technological support is given to the social networks. Knowledge reports are saved in Lotus Notes databases with an intranet shell around this. Nobody has any real idea of how these databases are used. The impression is that people only make use of the database when they are confronted with a new task.

The specialists communicate with one another primarily via e-mail. Participants hardly use the conferencing facilities at all. Unilever is still looking for an effective way of providing its communities with day-to-day support. An example of ICT support is the IceNet-intranet, which can be used by managers working in the ice-cream sector to exchange data with the entire company about the best working methods.

The involvement of senior management was essential for the success of knowledge management activities at Unilever. These initiatives were supported at a high level by the 'Senior Technology Director'. As mentioned earlier, the networks of senior management employees undoubtedly have a positive influence on the success of the knowledge workshops. A lot of time is required to attune the strategic and operational levels of the parallel operations with one another. Powers of persuasion are needed to clarify how knowledge workshops fit into a strategy.

The initiatives came into existence quite intuitively. The results such as the emergence of communities and individual learning were not foreseen. Unilever is now trying to capitalize on this.

Enablers
- Unilever's strategy
- support of senior management
- seniority of those taking the initiative
- knowledge-friendly culture
- affiliation with individual need
- people-driven

Potential risks
- mobilizing the support of the business unit
- affiliation with strategic and operational initiative
- continuity of communities
- tension between individual input and local responsibility
- competitive relationships between factories

5. KNOWLEDGE DEVELOPMENT VIA DIGITAL PLATFORMS AT THE MINISTRY OF HOUSING, SPATIAL PLANNING AND THE ENVIRONMENT

The Ministry of Housing, Spatial Planning and the Environment has several years of experience with developing knowledge through communities. These communities come together on the Internet via digital discussion platforms. As such they can be described as virtual communities. A description of experiences with these virtual communities teaches us how the Internet is used to make communities possible. The experiences are not always that positive and therefore provide us with insights into possible traps and ways in which we can avoid them.

Profile of the Ministry of Housing, Spatial Planning and the Environment

The mission of the Ministry is to ensure the lasting quality of the environment in which we live. In this instance 'lasting' means: 'leaving your children with the world as you yourself would wish to find it.'

It carries out this mission with approximately 4000 employees. The Ministry itself consists of the Government Architect's Office, the Director General's Staff Office and the central directorates which include: the Accommodation Policy Directorate, the Finance and Economics Directorate, the Design and Technology Directorate, the Project Management Directorate, the Internal Policy Directorate, and Account Management.

5.1 The knowledge initiative

The discussion platforms are an initiative within the framework of the National Action Programme (NAP). NAP is a joint initiative between several Dutch Ministries including the Ministry of Justice, the Ministry of Economic Affairs, the Ministry of Transport, Public Works and Water Management, the Ministry of Social Affairs, the Ministry of Education, Culture and Science, and the Ministry of Housing, Spatial Planning and the Environment. NAP's goal is to trace the relationship between government and modern information and communication technology. One of the spearheads was to stimulate the government to make greater use of the electronic superhighway. In response to this, the Ministry of Housing decided to set up a project to evaluate the role of ICT with regard to interactive policy development.

Discussion platforms[8]

The Ministry of Housing has been using digital discussion platforms to support and stimulate interactive policy development since 1996. Interactive policy development is a process of a sharing a common vision which is geared towards the execution of a common policy within a network consisting of players that are mutually dependent on one another. The distinguishing feature of this method of drawing up a plan is that citizens, end-users and other socially involved parties can all join in at an early stage and think about ideas and solutions. Furthermore, those taking the initiative also believe that the quality of decision-making is actually improved by including different relevant players.

Thanks to the platforms, the Ministry has a better grasp of the problems and aspirations of those involved, which in turn makes it possible to define the problem more sharply. At the same time the government can exploit the creativity and expertise of those taking part. People who work in a particular company for a long time increasingly begin to look at the world from the organization's perspective and way of thinking. Interactive images can free them from this type of blinkered vision and widen their horizons. Other advantages of interactive policy development include creating public support and bridging the gap between the government and citizens.

In order to acquire more experience with interactive policy development, since 1997 a few digital discussion platforms have been initiated and evaluated. In total, the Ministry has gained experience with ten discussion platforms, out of which seven have since been discontinued. Examples of platforms include NL2030 (concerning the future of the Netherlands), Environment and economics (concerning a possible synergy between both of them), the Sustainable Building project and Pegasus (an internal discussion platform). The discussion platforms have already gone beyond the experimental stage and are now a permanent feature within the Ministry's communication structure.

Whenever a project group is interested in initiating a digital discussion, it can always approach the PR and External Communication department at the Ministry and ask it to set up a platform. In practice it appears that the need for knowledge and new ideas about a specific theme is the most important reason for establishing the discussion platforms.

The objectives of discussion platforms have been formulated as follows:
- To encourage participation by the key players (individuals concerned about or interested in the subject) in the policy theme and to stimulate a dialogue between these players, the government and politicians.
- To provide information about the policy theme and insights into the specific policy process so that participation is facilitated at the right moment and with an equal level of knowledge.
- As a result of this, to increase the quality of and basis for the policy and the presentation of the policy to the outside world.

Internet makes discussions independent from time and space restrictions. This has a number of potential advantages[9]:

Potential for wide-ranging accessibility
During a non-digital debate, there are organizational limitations on the number of participants that can take part in the debate, while in principle an unlimited number of people can take part via the Internet. Through this the debate becomes more

diverse and participants come into contact with the views of people or bodies whom they might otherwise never have met.

Lowers the threshold for participation
Participants themselves can choose the moment that they wish to make a contribution and do not have to leave their premises to do so. In addition, there is also the option to participate anonymously, or partly anonymously (only giving one's position, sex and age). This can be particularly advantageous to directors, in situations where they wish to become involved in the discussion without causing the discussion to be directed to them alone.

Greater depth and reflection
During a debate an immediate response is usually required which means that the participants who think quickly and articulate their thoughts easily have the advantage. During a discussion via the Internet it is possible to take more time to reflect on how to articulate an argument.

Possibility for different lines of discussion
During a debate, sub-themes are usually dealt with in different groups due to lack of time. However, because a digital debate is not bound by the constraints of real time, participants can debate different subjects successively.

More polarity
During the course of a debate, social proximity generally results in participants starting to identify with the group and this, in turn, creates a tendency to negotiate and reach consensus. In a digital debate, however, there is no question of social proximity and so the discussion revolves more around the arguments. Another reason for this is the fact that power and status figure less prominently.

Organization of the discussion
Most discussion platforms are organized as follows. After setting up a website and inviting people or departments to react, a project leader places a new proposition on the platform every fortnight. The panel chairman proceeds to compile a weekly summary of the incoming reactions. The propositions are presented partly by the panel chairman - possibly on the basis of preceding reactions - and partly by the participants. A panel chairman (and initiator) with a supervisory role was chosen instead of a panel chairman who steers the process based on his or her extensive expertise. The project team provides support to the panel chairman regarding content.

The contributions seem to be very different with regard to theme, length and substance. For most platforms, relevant target groups were contacted in writing and invited to make a contribution. The contributions from the field involve supplying information, setting out the different points of view, commenting on the opinions of others, and providing solutions, requirements, hopes and aspirations and other ideas that hinge upon specific policy questions.

5.2 Experiences

The experiences that the Ministry has had with digital platforms have not always been positive[10]. An insight into these problems, therefore, can be edifying for others who are also interested in initiating digital discussion groups. Mostly it is the proposition that receives the responses, not the reactions of others to the proposition. Because of this the platforms are eventually reduced to resembling a mere list of opinions rather than a multilateral discussion. Through the absence of a true dialogue there is no question of reaching a consensus and the one-off viewpoints that have been put forward are not changed. Better control and moderating can alleviate this problem.

Employees at the Ministry seldom intervene in the content aspect of the discussion. This passive attitude occurs, among other reasons, because the Ministry's employees in general are not (yet) accustomed to using the Internet. In addition, the employees have problems with the role that they have to fulfil. A Ministry of Housing employee can have a clear personal opinion about, for example, the Sustainable Building project that is not consistent with the general opinion of the department. Anonymity, which by the way had already been discussed frequently, can alleviate this problem.

One of the objectives of the debate on the Internet is to continuously enrich the discussion. The problem is that it is not always easy to discern innovative elements in an argument that largely consists of defending a specific opinion. In addition, many contributions are worded in a long-winded and illogical way. It still demands time and effort to recognize original ideas in the course of such a raw discussion. The propositions are also often too general to provoke a real discussion. Besides, a number of panel chairs have remarked that most of the discussions involve pet subjects with which the project groups were already familiar.

Some panel chairs have problems coming to terms with the new ideas. As one panel chair put it:

> 'What can you actually do with all those creative noises?'

This has to do with the poor preparation of a discussion platform in particular. In some cases the results of the discussions are actually included in a final report.

The experiences with working with digital platforms at the Ministry of Housing show that this type of community needs to be strictly moderated. When this does not happen, the discussion devolves into a kind of electronic notice board. Personal ideas, viewpoints and conclusions about a common theme are publicized on this notice board, but no reactions to either these or preceding ideas are ever posted. In other words: electronic discussion platforms need to be moderated as soon as their objective becomes the reciprocal exchange of knowledge. The first platforms in particular suffered from the problem that very little attention was given to moderating them. This often means that a string of discussions exists on the website with no actual structure. This was taken into consideration with the later platforms. Some panel chairs for example give a summary of the arguments each week.

Apparently, a discussion platform 'lives' on average for only three weeks. After these three weeks the enthusiasm to join in ebbs away. This three-week lifespan seems to apply generally to all the platforms. The Sustainable Building project anticipated this and arranged for a real meeting a few weeks later. Participants in the discussion platform met each other face to face and this provided a stimulus for renewed, lively discussions. Generally speaking, participants in the different platforms often know each other. This presence of a personal network with shared knowledge, interests or concerns increases the chance of further discussions.

The Ministry uses the discussion platforms mostly in situations where they provide additional personal benefit to individual participants. In the discussion about the National Packages Sustainable Building project, for example, there are four contributing parties: people from the building trade, users (future residents), policy makers (from the Ministry) and researchers (from a technical university). The last group in particular generates most of the discussion. The most important reason for them to participate is not so much the exchange of knowledge in itself, but so that they can build up contacts and be part of a community in order to be given research projects.

More often than not, participants feel that they have landed in a playground rather than that their contribution has had any real effect. It is not made clear to them that their views on current or future policy are important for policy development. In addition, when the discussion platforms are discontinued no feedback occurs.

Support and interest from top management appears to be very important. In this way, the contribution of the then Minister for Housing, Spacial Planning and the Environment in the Netherlands gave an extra impetus to the discussion.

Enablers
- desire for interactive policy development
- support from the senior level within the Ministry
- moderators
- added value for the individual
- potential for widespread accessibility
- polarity of discussions
- combination of an electronic and physical meeting

Potential risks
- no physical access
- different hats of the civil servant and member of the public
- vaguely worded contributions
- unclear discussion structure
- list-making rather than interacting
- short lifespan of the discussions

6 DISCUSSION: THE COMMUNITY AS KNOWLEDGE PROVIDER

The three cases give, for many reasons, a very varied picture of the forms of knowledge-sharing within communities. Both Stork and the Ministry have chosen to structure networks to stimulate new developments by combining available internal and external knowledge. Unilever too is looking for forms of synergy by means of exchanging the knowledge that is present. At Unilever, it is firstly more a matter of disseminating and recording the available knowledge than developing new knowledge.

Table 8 gives an overview of the features of knowledge-sharing, as discussed in the case studies in this chapter.

Companies have different objectives with regard to knowledge-sharing. One objective that they do have in common with each other, however, is to develop knowledge with regard to future policy or innovation. This knowledge objective is a distraction from the strategic goals that the different organizations set themselves. Although the different organizations have shaped the creation of communities, barriers actually exist within the organization that prevents optimal use being made of this knowledge-sharing.

The Ministry of Housing has problems interpreting and adapting the relevance of the new knowledge. Stork on the other hand has problems getting the results to be accepted. This is mainly because it is a very decentralized organization made up of many companies that each have their own identity. Knowledge derived from a centralized structure such as the IPI will not be accepted by everyone or will not be considered to be relevant to his or her own company. Unilever has the problem that the knowledge database containing the knowledge that flows from the knowledge workshops is seldom consulted. The real question is whether the community members perceive this as a problem. Due to the fact that the workshop participants already obtain knowledge from each other during the course of the workshop itself, they look upon the recorded knowledge as being superfluous.

Table 8. Features of practical situations

Learning process	Stork	Unilever	Ministry of Housing
Main objective	Fresh insights	To exchange and develop knowledge	Interactive policy development
Role of ICT	Reports on a diskette	Knowledge mapping, Lotus Notes	Digital discussion platform
Relevance of ICT	Marginal	Present but not essential	Essential
Worker profile	Specialists, managers	Experts	Policy staff, interested parties, and those outside the organization who have an interest
Type of learning process	Exchanging knowledge in order to generate new ideas	Exchanging knowledge for the benefit of development	Exchanging knowledge for the purpose of creating new policy
Support for the learning process	Workgroups	Knowledge workshops	Virtual community
Experiences	The structure appears to rely on seniority. The results are assimilated in a haphazard fashion.	When acknowledgement, status and physical meetings are combined this accelerates the formation of 'communities'	Virtual communities fall short of the mark if they lack clear objectives and are not managed properly.

One important aspect that distinguishes knowledge-sharing in these communities from knowledge-sharing in other inter-relationships is that the *process* of knowledge-sharing seems to be more important than the *result*. 'Pleasure' is a key word for those participating in the digital platforms of the Ministry. The majority of the participants mainly seem to take part in the discussion because communication via the Internet is experienced as something new and exciting. A closer analysis of the number of participants revealed, for example, that the distribution did not seem to be as wide as the number of discussions that had taken place would suggest. Often it was simply a small group of active individuals who enjoyed communicating via the Internet. Members of the workshops at Unilever also enjoyed being part of the programme. People really enjoyed spending a week in an exotic environment sharing knowledge about, for example, tomato sauce with colleagues from all over the world. Members of the IPI at Stork too reported on the pleasures of meeting colleagues whom they usually do not meet and discussing innovative topics.

The role of ICT
ICT plays a role in knowledge development at both Unilever and the Ministry of Housing. As we can already denote in the description of professional organizations and organizations that follow routine procedures, ICT can be an excellent aid to develop individual knowledge, such as in the Postbank's learning environment. Other types of ICT support are required to facilitate knowledge development in which employees create new knowledge by interacting with one another. A glowing picture of all the possibilities is given in the literature. ICT's contribution to knowledge development can be found in its support of the communication between individuals. GroupWare applications such as electronic communities, video conferencing and 'group discussion rooms' are often considered crucial (Blackler 1995). These applications facilitate key processes within organizations such as communication and teamwork.

The constructions with which Unilever works are, in a certain sense, traditional for 'knowledge-mapping'. Unilever came to the conclusion that ICT can only support specific operations. In this way the knowledge workshops make intensive use of software tools to facilitate the process of knowledge-sharing and archiving. The communities also use an intranet. Nevertheless, Unilever derives the most benefit from direct face-to-face interaction. The discussions via the intranet offer possibilities, but do not (yet) effectively lead to knowledge development because they go on asynchronously.

Knowledge work
What is characteristic of the knowledge work in the case studies described is that people are focussed on knowledge development. Development can be geared towards products and operations or even policy development, as in the case of the Ministry of Housing. One contribution to successful knowledge development is that people can discern their own advantages from the contribution that they make. They recognize a win-win situation.

Stork and Unilever have created an inherent potential tension with their IPI and knowledge workshops. The contribution that these knowledge workers make to the knowledge development of the organization does not need to be appreciated on the operational level. It is therefore also important that it is explicitly appreciated at the highest level.

The existence of communities is dependent on the need perceived by the individual members for social interaction. For example, at the Ministry of Housing the 'electronic communities' are only granted an average lifespan of three weeks because people do not meet each other 'face to face'. As a result, communication stays on a superficial level. Typical for knowledge work and knowledge development is the importance of personal encounters. People develop knowledge during these encounters.

The different working groups at Stork have been in existence for years, partly because these communities have been given the appearance of a personal network. Meetings of members of the working groups are largely used for networking, for lobbying and for other forms of unstructured knowledge-sharing. This has to do, in particular, with the personal additional benefits that employees obtain by being members of such a network. Exchanging knowledge among colleagues who are operating far and wide is - apart from being functional - also simply enjoyable.

Learning in communities
The aim of knowledge-sharing at Stork, the Ministry of Housing, and Unilever is ultimately to develop knowledge that will result in new operations, new policy, new products and even new factories. Stork's working groups, Unilever's communities and the virtual platforms of the Ministry of Housing successfully learn from and with each other by sharing knowledge. However, only Unilever has been successful in transforming this knowledge into organizational knowledge. Objectifying knowledge and transforming shared knowledge into organizational knowledge occurs along two lines at Unilever. On the one hand, Unilever records knowledge in databases, on the other it creates communities in which knowledge disseminates itself.

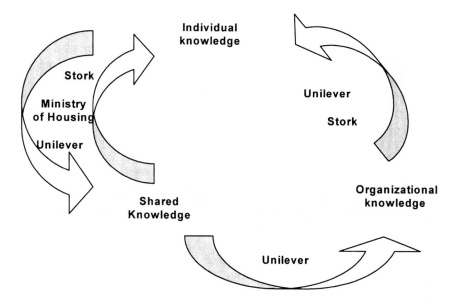

Figure 11. Learning processes in communities

Communities are highly informal associations for knowledge exchange. Shell, Unilever and Stork illustrate the strength of the different communities by facilitating individual and organizational learning. Communities provide management with enormous challenges. They are often dependent on an initiator and stimulator that has to fulfil specific conditions. The lifespan of the communities depends on the concerns of the individual members. This makes them hard to latch onto as management tools. For example, at Unilever it is uncertain how long the communities will continue to exist. For the time being the enthusiasm among those involved would tend to indicate a long-lasting life.

Communities are hard to control given that the development of situated knowledge is often not planned and takes place unconsciously. Managers focus on formalized work and learning operations and are therefore not always aware of the knowledge development that takes place during day-to-day interactions. Not all daily interactions between knowledge workers or experts instantly result in communities. Characteristically, there is a mutual need and concern for knowledge-sharing. Project teams can, for example, operate as a temporary community. Mapping out all the communities in order to manage the knowledge is an impossible task. Participants and input change on a regular basis and recording all of this is just an instant snapshot that can become obsolete within a day. Sometimes even the community members themselves are not aware of their collective learning processes, which makes managing them even more complicated (Ciborra and Lanzara 1993). In view of the fact that working and learning are so closely interwoven with one another and that learning takes place as part of the daily work operations, people are often impervious to the changes brought about by their actions (Brown and Duguid 1992).

These managerial dilemmas notwithstanding, we do believe that communities provide the most suitable organizing structures to support learning in organizations. We will discuss this assumption in more detail in the final chapter of this book.

7. SUMMARY

In this chapter three organizations that have each established communities were discussed from their own unique perspective: Stork, Unilever, and the Ministry of Housing. Knowledge development in communities was the central theme. It was found that a moderator is necessary to stimulate knowledge development in a community. In addition, communities appear to function well if they are created from the bottom-up. People take part in them on a voluntary basis. It must be clear that participation fulfils a mutual need. Stimulating communities has a highly process oriented dimension. The result is often less important than the process of knowledge-sharing amongst individuals. In order to develop the process well personal encounters where people meet face to face are important. Communities do not exist thanks to ICT, but ICT might offer good support to communities;

especially where people or groups who are distributed over a wide geographical area are concerned.

PART 3

A CRITICAL ANALYSIS

In the following three chapters we critically analyse the practices described in part two of the book. We do this by analysing the various knowledge-sharing practices while asking the following six research questions:

- When is knowledge shared?

- Why is knowledge shared?

- Who shares knowledge?

- Where is knowledge shared?

- How is knowledge shared?

- Which knowledge is shared?

Addressing these exploratory research questions brings three basic critical aspects of knowledge-sharing to the fore (see figure 12):

- Managing knowledge-sharing

- Learning from knowledge-sharing

- (ICT) support for knowledge-sharing

The practices show that if no attention or inadequate attention is paid to these three aspects then more often than not this will hinder rather than stimulate the institutionalization of knowledge-sharing. In the next three chapters the following traps will be discussed:

- *The management trap*

- *The individual learning trap*

- *The ICT trap.*

126

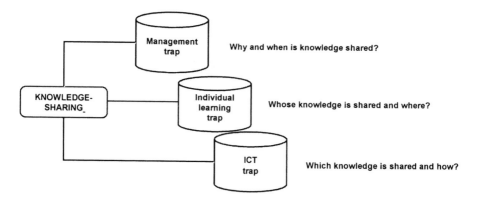

Figure 12. Different traps in knowledge sharing

We will argue that organizations might face problems when they treat the management of knowledge-sharing:

— from a managerial perspective without paying attention to the real - individual and group - needs to share their knowledge;

— as being related to individual learning without paying attention to the learning of the organization as a whole;

— from a technological approach without paying attention to social interaction.

These traps should be considered as potential risks. Risk can be avoided, as many organizations have shown over the years. Consequently, next to a critical analysis of the origins and consequences of these traps, we will discuss how these traps might be avoided.

CHAPTER 7

THE MANAGEMENT TRAP

1. INTRODUCTION

Whenever we ask the question "When is knowledge shared?", we notice that in almost all the companies that were researched management plays a proactive role. Proactive in this context means that organizations initiate knowledge-sharing based in particular on the opportunities that they see for themselves. Initiatives for knowledge-sharing are often based on the idea that this will create opportunities rather than on the idea that they fit in with a predominant need or problem situation.

The role of management in knowledge-sharing also comes to the fore when we ask the question 'Why is knowledge shared?" We saw that in most of the researched organizations, management plays not only a proactive but also a relatively dominant role in initiating knowledge-sharing practices. Dominant here means that companies view knowledge management primarily from a managerial perspective. It is often more important for the company to share knowledge than for the knowledge workers themselves.

Both management roles – proactive and dominant – increase the risk that knowledge-sharing practices will not last any longer than it takes to gain explicit organizational and managerial support. In other words, the role of management in supporting knowledge-sharing does not contribute successfully to the institutionalization or routinization of knowledge-sharing. This is why we label this risk 'the management trap'.

Both potential risks that make up this management trap influence each other. This is even more so with regard to its consequences. Because of the proactive and dominant role of management, knowledge-sharing initiatives supported or introduced by management seldom match the individual and group needs to share knowledge. In this chapter, we will discuss possible ways to avoid these risks. In order to adapt better to existing knowledge-sharing needs, we will pay attention to the conditions in which individuals and groups feel the need for and are prepared to share knowledge. We will also discuss how situations can be created in which voluntary knowledge-sharing might occur.

The consequences of the management traps can be discussed in one section: namely adapting to individual needs to share knowledge. The reasons behind it however call for a separate, independent discussion about the proactive and dominant managerial role. Consequently, we will first tackle the danger of focussing knowledge-sharing too much on future opportunities and too little on the problems and needs that exist at that moment. We will link the reasons behind proactive management to the three theoretical approaches on knowledge management as discussed in chapter 2. We will go on to discuss the risk of organizations defining knowledge-sharing mainly in the context of management needs, without giving much attention to any additional benefits that might be derived for the individual knowledge worker. These analyses lead to a number of guidelines to stimulate the need for knowledge-sharing among knowledge workers and link these to the organization's needs.

2. PROACTIVE MANAGEMENT

When one narrows it down, there are two reasons for management to initiate the structuring of knowledge-sharing: problem solving initiatives and initiatives that generate opportunities. Both initiatives strongly overlap with each other. Opportunity generating initiatives are often explained as initiatives that solve existing problems although in practice they are mainly proactive rather than reactive.

In our study the opportunity generating initiatives (Table 2, chapter 1) all used the explicit label 'knowledge management'. These initiatives were all introduced based on different reasons:

- the efficiency of knowledge-sharing;

- the financial-economic value of the knowledge factor;

- the additional benefits of ICT applications.

When we review the literature on knowledge management it appears that these reasons confirm the three basic reasons for introducing knowledge management. In fact, these three reasons comply with the three theoretical approaches of knowledge-management, as discussed in *Chapter 2*: the process approach, the intellectual capital approach and the technical approach.

The efficiency of knowledge-sharing.
Much has been said and written about knowledge management in the past few years. The ideal scenario is when knowledge management provides an organization in which knowledge flows freely. Such an organization does not needlessly duplicate activities and does not suffer any damage when employees leave. Senior

management has access via ICT tools to its main production factor: knowledge. Such an ideal organization is worth striving for in the eyes of many managers. Therefore, it is understandable that they feel ill at ease when their organization does not participate in any form of knowledge management. In this way, managers increasingly feel the need to centralize and publicize scattered and often implicit knowledge. This is even more pertinent when the wheel is being re-invented in different parts of the organization. It was for these reasons in particular that Schiphol's knowledge-sharing initiatives were launched.

The financial-economic value of the knowledge factor.
Another important reason to invest in knowledge-sharing is suggested by the growing awareness of the financial-economic importance of knowledge. Organizations realize that an insight into existing knowledge contributes to the organization's success and even its ability to compete. Many publications illustrate that the organization's intellectual capital is usually worth much more than its intrinsic value (Bontis 1999, Edvinsson and Malone 1997, Roos et al 1998, Stewart 1997, Sveiby 1997). Top management and shareholders are becoming increasingly aware that core competences and the competitive ability of an organization are embedded in the (implicit) shared knowledge of the organization's members. Of the companies that we researched, IBM in particular is a good example of where the management of intellectual capital is a reason to introduce knowledge management.

The added value of ICT applications
Initiatives that create opportunities often originate from the potential that ICT offers to initiate, manage, follow and stimulate knowledge-sharing within the organization. The very concept of 'knowledge management' was first coined in the ICT environment. Because of this, at the beginning of and throughout the 1990s, attention was especially focussed on the technical side. The birth and growth of ICT applications such as knowledge systems, Lotus Notes, intranet and artificial intelligence offered new possibilities to improve the structure of knowledge within the organization. More recently e-business initiatives spurred organizations on to make their internal knowledge available to customers, and e-learning enhanced knowledge management initiatives. A large part of knowledge-sharing practices is primarily ICT driven. In Chapter 9 we will explore in more depth the possible risks inherent in ICT-centric approaches.

These opportunity-creating initiatives are most often products of organizational imitation (see box). Managers are quick to feel that they are falling behind if they do not go along with a new organizational perspective (Abrahamson 1996, Kiesler 1997). In this situation, organizations introduce knowledge management because they are stimulated by stories from other organizations who proclaim that they are successfully executing knowledge management (Scarbrough and Swan 2001). Conferences and workshops are an ideal platform for 'best practices' which are often introduced by enthusiastic knowledge managers.

Organizational imitation

Powell and Dimaggio (1991) distinguish three forces that trigger processes of organizational imitation: coercion, mimicry, and normative pressures. Coercion refers to a process of diffusion that is more or less imperative. Coercive imitation results from being dependent on other organizations as well as from cultural expectations in the society within which organizations function. Mimicry refers to a process of diffusion that is triggered by an explicit desire to copy others. Organizations frequently model themselves on other organizations when technologies are poorly understood, when goals are ambiguous or when the environment creates symbolic uncertainty (March 1988). Normative imitation is less conscious and often stems from professionalization. Levitt and March (1988) refer to normative pressures culminating in a two-stage diffusion process involving 'the spread of a disease within a small group by contagion and then by broadcasting from them to the remainder of a population'. Examples are knowledge diffused through educational institutions, through experts, through personnel selections, through management books, and consultancy.

One danger of imitation is lurking in the background here. Managers frequently base their case on conceptual images or on fresh but limited experience with projects. This is further enhanced as many of the published case studies on knowledge management are either conceptual or based on such project experiences. In addition, there is also the danger that positive stories cover up more negative experiences and traps.

Another danger when imitating is that the concepts are not tuned in to the specific situation within each of the organizations. Interviewees in our research often referred to the same knowledge management books and the same 'best practices'[11] (such as British Petroleum, see box). Much of the practical experience gained with knowledge management initiatives are sticky to diffuse (Szulanski 1996). Knowledge management must not end up being viewed as a standard method with standard guidelines. Each organization needs its own interpretation furnished by the requirements made by that particular organization.

The success story of British Petroleum

British Petroleum allows knowledge-sharing to take place in virtual teams before, during and after a project. These 'communities' determine which generic and specific 'best practices' can be identified. The lessons are made available on the Intranet where information on some ten thousand BP-employees and their specific know-how can also be found.

British Petroleum has shown that knowledge management initiatives that stem from a specific company need, can produce substantial profits. Estimates have been made at roundabout 350 million dollars.

Many companies hold up this form of knowledge-sharing as an example. Competitors of BP such as Shell and Esso are working on similar initiatives but will not allow themselves to be drawn on the results that they have had so far.

What is striking in our study is that where knowledge-sharing has been introduced in order to create opportunities, this has either been in organizations that have encountered serious problems (ING Barings, Cap Gemini and the Ministry) or in organizations that have up till now not come up with any results (Schiphol and Corus, formerly Hoogovens.).

During our study we also encountered problem-solving initiatives. These initiatives focussed on a concrete problem for which the structuring of knowledge-sharing was seen as a solution. NN is a good example. Due to the internal reorganization from product-driven to market-driven services, NN considered it necessary to capture the knowledge that already existed and make it accessible for others. At the Postbank too, it was an internal reorganization that led to an improved structure being built for knowledge-sharing. At Stork and Unilever it was arguments about efficiency problems caused by the geographically distributed locations of the different companies and branches that led to structured forms of knowledge-sharing being introduced. What is striking is that all the initiatives that stemmed from a problem-solving motive were only given the knowledge management label much later.

A premature conclusion would be to reject a proactive approach to knowledge-sharing. However, this would be unwise as initiatives that are introduced to create opportunities can also lead to fruitful knowledge-sharing practices. Nevertheless, it is certainly important that the organization remains focussed on the existing needs for knowledge-sharing within the organization. In the following paragraph we will come back to this.

3. KNOWLEDGE-SHARING FROM A MANAGEMENT PERSPECTIVE

If the organization definitely wants to reap the fruits from knowledge-sharing practices, that is to say: if it wishes to learn from the knowledge present in the organization, then more is needed than simply adapting to the existing needs. Initiatives for knowledge-sharing are vulnerable when the need for knowledge-sharing between knowledge workers is not explicitly part of the organizational needs to introduce knowledge-sharing practices. Here we clash with the second danger in the management trap category: knowledge-sharing viewed exclusively from a managerial perspective.

An important risk when managing knowledge-sharing is the one-sided emphasis of the need for knowledge-sharing. Structuring knowledge management processes is specifically looked upon as a management issue. In general, initiating structured forms of knowledge-sharing produces more advantages for management than for the employees who share knowledge in practice.

Supporting knowledge-sharing by means of an intranet often provides an example of a dominant management approach. Initiatives to record experiences in a database so that others might draw from these experiences are inspired mainly by management. This type of construction can indeed have interesting benefits at an organizational level. In practice, the usual reserve concerning recording experiences generally prevails while its additional benefits are not clear.

For example, ING Barings' Head Office considered it vitally important to build an intranet which logged the knowledge from all its branches throughout the world. The idea behind this was that whenever someone from the head offices had to travel to a branch elsewhere, he or she could look up the required knowledge, just before they set off. This could be knowledge for example about the country, the branch, the most important clients or the key prices. This was clearly a situation based on the needs of the head office managers. There was no obvious need for the individual employees at the various local offices to provide the knowledge that the head office needed. ING Barings, therefore, had great difficulty gathering knowledge from the different countries.

Management is completely dependent on the involvement of the knowledge workers. As long as no attention is paid to the advantages that employees would gain if they shared their knowledge, then knowledge-sharing initiatives will continue to have little effect. For successful knowledge-sharing it is necessary that managers are certain that the knowledge-sharing initiative is seen as being beneficial to both the organization and the knowledge worker. Management cannot enforce knowledge-sharing. All this might sound trivial, yet during our study we saw different cases where such a win-win situation was clearly absent.

Some of the knowledge-sharing practices that we studied did provide an added value for the employees. In some cases the employees themselves accredited this added value. Unilever for example, started its workshops from a management perspective. The idea of distilling knowledge, and then centralizing and publicizing it was the main reason to arrange for people from all over the world to come together in order to share their knowledge. After a while, the employees gave the initiative their own added value. The main objective of the workshop now is to create 'communities of practice' where people voluntarily both generate and share knowledge with one another.

The employees launch initiatives too, while the additional value to the organization only becomes apparent at a later stage. This was the case at Netherlands Railways, for example, where a conductor took the initiative to develop the RailPocket. At a later stage the organization recognized the value of this initiative and introduced the tool throughout the entire organization.

The perceived value for management does not necessarily have to be the same as that of the knowledge workers. A win-win situation can also occur when players take part in knowledge management for different reasons. For example, the Ministry of Housing launched the electronic discussion list for the Sustainable Buildings project in order to better adapt the policy development in this area to the wishes and ideas of different experts and concerned parties. The reason for the employees at the Ministry to take part was to get discussions off the ground, to rethink what was happening in the 'field' and to come up with new ideas. Researchers at a department of architecture at one of the universities were important partners in the discussion. Their most important motivation for taking part in the discussion was primarily the possibility of attracting new research projects.

There are different reasons why people are not prepared, or not able, to exchange their knowledge with others. In the following sections we discuss the obstacles to knowledge exchange that we encountered in the companies we studied, as well as in the literature.

4. PSYCHOLOGICAL OBSTACLES TO EXCHANGING KNOWLEDGE

Lack of trust.
A lack of trust amongst peers is often pointed to as an obstacle to knowledge-sharing (e.g. Davenport and Prusak 1998, Dixon 1999) Employees will not simply share their knowledge at the drop of a hat. There has to be a level of trust present that reassures them that the shared knowledge is in good hands. Confidence that the knowledge-sharing is a case of 'give and take' is necessary. In fact, going one step further than an absence of trust: not trusting one another makes knowledge-sharing completely impossible. In each organization we studied, a certain level of trust was present.

Relinquishing power.
If knowledge is power, then sharing knowledge must mean giving away accumulated power. In the literature, giving away power is seen, alongside trust, as the most important problem in knowledge-sharing. (e.g. Davenport and Prusak 1998, Weggeman 1997). However, we did not encounter this argument in our study. What we did come across was that some individuals would rather not make their knowledge public property because this heightens their vulnerability. This therefore particularly concerns individuals who have reason to doubt the public value of the knowledge that they have amassed.

Lack of time.
Whenever knowledge-sharing demands extra effort, lack of time is often given as a reason to refrain from knowledge-sharing. In this way, employees at Corus, IBM and Cap Gemini feel that adding their project experiences to the knowledge base

would take up too much of their time and requires too much discipline, no doubt because new projects quickly beckon. Reflecting on experiences acquired during the previous project is seen as tiresome and inefficient. Consultants at Cap Gemini in particular, who are paid by the hour, consider posting their experiences to a system to be too time-consuming.

Lack of matching support facilities.
In practice the actual need for knowledge-sharing does not receive the correct – technical or social – support. This particularly applies to the use of ICT tools, which calls for knowledge to be made explicit. We see this at IBM, for example, where employees have difficulty making the learning experience they have acquired explicit. For the potential knowledge receiver too, there are pockets of resistance to using ICT tools for knowledge-sharing. This resistance has to do with the fact that knowledge cannot easily be extracted from the carrier. People want to know from whom they learn as this provides important 'meta-knowledge'. Knowledge only has meaning if it can be related to people (Brown and Duguid 2000b). This is one of the reasons why knowledge that has been recorded in knowledge files seldom leads to the knowledge being reused. This means that aids to knowledge-sharing such as intranets and knowledge bases that are geared towards codifying knowledge, are not effective enough. When sharing experiences, people prefer to look for support from personal networks rather than electronic networks. We will look at this in greater detail in Chapter 9.

Solitariness
Solitariness inhibits knowledge-sharing. Solitariness can be the result of geographical distribution, professionalism or a lack of peer group and organizational involvement. For example, there is an absence of knowledge-sharing at the Netherlands Railways because the profession and mobility of the conductors leads to isolation. The need for knowledge-sharing is really felt at the moment when other peers become involved. At the railways we see this happening, for example, during strikes and work disruptions. Attention for the non-knowledge-sharing professional is not new (Argyris 1990, Weggeman 1997). Many professionals have either little or no need to share knowledge. In addition, people often do not want to use another person's experiences. For this reason, software engineers at IBM would prefer to find their own solutions rather than take on the solutions that have been arrived at by others.

The success of knowledge-sharing thus depends on the willingness to participate. We encountered different reasons for this such as expanding the effectiveness and efficiency of work (at the Railways and the Postbank), acquiring status by being considered an expert (NN), making work more pleasant (Unilever), and coming into contact with other people (Stork, Unilever and the Ministry). We will discuss these and other possibilities to increase the need for knowledge-sharing in the next section.

5. FIGHTING THE MANAGEMENT TRAP: INCREASE THE NEED FOR KNOWLEDGE-SHARING

What lessons can be learned from the individual cases that go beyond the specific character of an organization? In this section we take experiences from the study as our point of reference, while we link these wherever possible to the various guidelines offered by the literature.

The balance between initiatives that generate opportunities and problem-solving initiatives

The management trap can be avoided by addressing the question on whether the initiatives comply with both the organizational as well as the individual's needs. Organizations would do well to find a balance between proactive and reactive knowledge management. Even when the temptation to implement knowledge management straight away is high, finding a balance first requires self-reflection. This implies that before introducing the initiative, management should first analyse both the current and future needs for knowledge management within the organization. The organizational learning model that we present in this book is also a useful tool in this respect. This analysis will likely lead to both an adaptation of the existing methods of knowledge-sharing as well as adaptation by the organization.

Interdependence and involvement in the organization

Some organizations assume that their employees' peer involvement and involvement in the organization can be increased by initiating reciprocal learning processes. One example of this is the creation of the master-apprentice situation where a senior staff member helps a newcomer to learn the tricks of the trade. Another way of stimulating peer involvement is by setting up 'competence centres' where presentations and courses can be given to colleagues. Although these and other conditions might stimulate knowledge-sharing in theory, they will only help if there is indeed a willingness to put some effort into somebody else's learning process. This pre-condition to knowledge-sharing is often missing. Fortunately, there are organizations where interdependence and involvement are 'normal'. In this type of situation dependency, loyalty and trust are the most important motives for knowledge-sharing. Such situations can call up the need for knowledge-sharing so strongly that factors that hinder knowledge-sharing, such as lack of time, insufficient facilities and isolation, have no influence. Examples of such are the following:

Mission-driven organizations

In strongly mission-driven organizations, such as Greenpeace or the World Bank, individual employees recognize the need for their work to contribute to the fulfilment of the organizational mission. The individual is governed by the needs of the organization. Through this, the individual is less likely to keep individually accumulated knowledge to him or herself. Knowledge-sharing has then reached the stage of being in the interests of both the individual and the organization.

People with a shared passion
The same applies to situations where there is a common cause. This is the case, for example, among the members of the workshops organized by Unilever Research. Participants are people with a passion for the profession. The discussions continue throughout the night at the bar. The shared interests make it easy to stimulate knowledge exchange and to overcome any clashes, for example as a result of cultural differences, that might arise otherwise.

Organizations in crisis situations
Organizations that find themselves in a specific crisis situation are sometimes also characterized by a (temporary) voluntary exchange of knowledge. Here, we should think of situations where the feeling of needing each other is stimulated. The launching stage of an organization is a good example of this, as is the moment that an organization threatens to go bankrupt (Miles and Randolf 1980).[12]

Companies that do not fulfil these criteria can still learn despite this - although it would not be sensible to deliberately call up crisis situations to stimulate knowledge-sharing. For example, organizations would do well to ask themselves whether their mission is inspiring enough for the knowledge workers to contribute to it. Unilever's workshop example can inspire organizations to organize meetings so that people with the same interest who, normally speaking, would work far away from one another, could meet and be able to share their knowledge. One single week, rather than part of the day or a meeting, seems to be more appropriate. The participants would then have the time to learn from each other and to develop a feeling of interdependence and mutual trust.

Mutuality and collective involvement can be enhanced by investing more in social capital than in human capital (see box). In the closing chapter of this book, we will discuss in more detail how companies can invest in social capital.

> **Social capital**
> Social scientists in several fields have suggested a common framework for understanding phenomena such as collective involvement and social bonding, a framework that is founded on the concept of social capital (Coleman 1988, 1990; Granovetter, 1985, Jacobs 1961, Putnam 1993). Social capital refers to those stocks of social trust; norms (mutual reciprocity) and networks that people can draw upon to solve common problems. By analogy with notions of physical capital and human capital - tools and training that enhance individual productivity – 'social capital' refers to features of social organization such as networks, norms, and social trust that facilitate coordination and cooperation for mutual benefit (Cohen and Prusak 2000). It has now become recognized that the 'traditional' types of capital (natural, physical and human) only partially determine the process of economic growth because they overlook the way in which

the economic actors interact and organize themselves to generate growth and development. The missing link is social capital.

Rewards of knowledge-sharing
One of the most complex issues in knowledge management initiatives is the extent to which people should be financially rewarded in order to encourage them to contribute to knowledge-sharing (Davenport and Prusak 1998). Rewards can take the form of money as well as the opportunity to take part in prestigious projects or by granting a special status. Generally speaking, financial rewards only have a short-term effect. Such direct explicit rewards can only stimulate people to actively participate in knowledge-sharing initiatives during the initial phase, but will not create a culture in which knowledge-sharing is part of the daily routine.

In practice, we see that companies such as IBM and Cap Gemini are considering whether to make an employee's contribution to knowledge-sharing part of their job performance evaluation or appraisal system. The effect of this type of stimulus is still uncertain. Most organizations still lack real experience in how to reward knowledge-sharing.

Other than financial rewards, there are also people-oriented measures such as acknowledgement and recognition. This is the case at NN who rewards its employees by giving status to those who have, over the years, demonstrated their willingness to help others. They may be considered for the position of Specialist within NN. At Stork too, the chance to take part in IPI is seen by many as an elevation of their status. Being chosen as an expert for the knowledge workshops at Unilever also provides a stimulus to share knowledge.

Sometimes companies attempt to motivate people with small gestures. Other companies give out new laptops and weekends in luxurious holiday resorts for the knowledge sharers. Coming up with new sources of inspiration appears to be a constant challenge. These stimuli in the meantime do not stop people viewing knowledge-sharing as an extra burden. These short term rewards fall short of instilling a routine approach to knowledge-sharing whereby knowledge-sharing simply becomes part of the employees' day-to-day thinking and actions.

In short, management should approach the issue of rewarding knowledge-sharing very carefully. Explicit rewards such as financial perks are basically compensations for the absence of voluntary knowledge-sharing. Up to now the best option seems to incorporate knowledge-sharing in the periodic performance evaluations, as is the case at IBM. Through this, people are regularly made aware of the need to help others and see the benefits of doing so. The hope is that knowledge-sharing will become routine in the long term.

Knowledge-friendly culture
Different companies have pointed out the importance of a knowledge-friendly culture. At the same time, they recognize that this is one of the complicating factors. This in itself is not a surprising observation as the culture of an organization has been described as a crucial factor in all types of transformation processes (Schein 1992).

Many knowledge management authors are still pessimistic about a knowledge-friendly culture being seen as a condition for successful knowledge management (Davenport and Prusak 1998). If a knowledge-friendly culture does not already exist then no technology or project management will help with this, goes the general view. It is virtually impossible to steer an organization's culture deliberately (and preferably as quickly as possible).

Yet there is some leeway to steer an organization's culture, although the effect will only be visible in the long term. By means of a personnel policy, one can explicitly take the building up of a knowledge-friendly culture into account. This can be done for example by hiring and promoting active knowledge sharers. As mentioned earlier, such a culture can also be built up through periodical assessments. We learn from Cap Gemini and IBM that it is possible to develop a culture by focussing attention on creating a pattern of norms and values through which self-management arises. The 'Master of your own Destiny' philosophy at IBM and Cap Gemini's 'win-execute-team' slogan prove this. In addition, it is important that enough possibilities for further growth are created. Standing still always means that little need is felt for knowledge-sharing.

One of the most critical factors in allowing a knowledge-friendly culture to develop is the attitude of management. Management has to set a pointed example by stimulating knowledge-sharing. This is not just with regard to what they say, but indeed how they behave. We will return to this in greater detail in the following chapter.

Avoiding too much time pressure
At different organizations time pressure seems to be a problem that stands in the way of motivating people to share knowledge. Filling out time sheets in project organizations can have a negative impact on knowledge-sharing. People experience pressure when they take part in projects. We see this happening for example when project evaluations, as part of standard project methodology, are missing. People have to become involved in new projects without having time to reflect on the past and to make their experiences available to others.

The guideline stating that it is management's responsibility to arrange for time to be made available certainly does not mean much during a boom time. People have to recognize the benefits of knowledge-sharing themselves and the company should positively value the effort. It is important that employees view the practice of knowledge-sharing as an important facet of their work. If not, knowledge-sharing is experienced as an extra pressure and this does not guarantee the knowledge-sharing initiative a long life. Or as Prusak puts it:

'It's when you ask people to add to their work burden without a *quid pro quo* that they resent it'.

Making knowledge about knowledge available
So far, many publications about knowledge management have kept quiet, strikingly enough, about the experienced value of knowledge. It is as if knowledge is objective and is valued as such: 'Put somebody else's knowledge in a file, make it public and everyone will enjoy it'. This rarely works in practice. The potential user first wants to know if 'it works', under which conditions using knowledge has an effect, what the hidden disadvantages of using knowledge are and how you should use the knowledge. Juicy stories are important sources of information for others to determine whether to use it in the future. To get a better understanding of this, people want to get to know the person behind the knowledge. Knowledge is closely linked up with the individual. If you do not like that person, then you will not readily be inclined to make use of his or her experiences.

A consultant at Cap Gemini stated that he sometimes consulted stored project reports when he had to supervise a similar project. The most important information for him was *who* had carried out the project and not *how* the project was carried out. With that information in hand, he then contacted the person concerned in order to subsequently relay experiences in a private conversation and exchange knowledge. In Chapter 9 we will return to this limited use of an intranet.

Knowledge about knowledge or 'meta-knowledge' cannot be logged in files, but rather flows through personal discussions. The exchange of this personal meta-knowledge thrives best in social networks or other structures to support social interaction, such as teacher-pupil relationships and communities. In social networks the reuse of knowledge goes more smoothly because the person behind the knowledge is known, the 'ins and outs' are known, it is geared more towards acquiring knowledge and there is a greater willingness to put energy into supporting someone else's learning processes (Brown and Duguid, 2000). Through the regular personal contact that takes place, a certain form of group bonding exists. Group bonding reduces the chance for mistrust, power and control; important obstacles to knowledge-sharing.

Senior people and experts
One way of stimulating knowledge-sharing is by giving senior people and experts a prominent place as a knowledge provider. Through their many years' experience their knowledge is often greatly valued and because of this more quickly absorbed by others. Unilever only brings people together in workshops if have many years'

working experience with a specific product or operation. Unilever deliberately chooses not to invite the young, career-minded and ambitious employees to the workshop. The input of senior staff members and experts increases the chance that the experiences that they contribute will be accepted.

At NN it is the experienced claims agents who are asked to play an active role in the knowledge management process. In their eyes such a formal task means nothing more than consolidating the informal role of expert and walking encyclopaedia that they have been playing for years. Their experience and seniority arouses a certain degree of trust, which results in them being consulted for advice and information more often than the knowledge base.

Senior staff members and experts can also stimulate the collective acceptance of knowledge in a more indirect way. In this way, they can play a more active role as 'jury' in evaluating knowledge that is intended for reuse. This occurs, for example, at IBM where a committee of experts records the knowledge in the form of 'best practices' in the knowledge base, so that this knowledge can be used again within the organization.

6. SUMMARY

When we ask questions such as why knowledge is shared and when it is shared, the answers obtained are important to management. Knowledge is shared in order to make optimal use of the knowledge that is scattered throughout an organization. Knowledge is shared to plug the gaps that exist due to employees' mobility and to create new ideas. Knowledge is also shared to stimulate new knowledge to be developed. All these reasons are based especially on management initiatives and play an important role in the introduction of knowledge-sharing in the organizations that we researched. However, many companies thereby overlook the fact that they are completely dependent upon the contribution of the individual to knowledge-sharing. Until knowledge-sharing is looked at from the point of view of the individual, knowledge-sharing initiatives will be doomed to have a short lifespan.

In this chapter we gave a number of guidelines on how to avoid these traps. These concerned, in particular, methods to increase the need for knowledge-sharing as well as to remove any obstacles in the way of knowledge-sharing. All these methods are based on the conviction that people are willing to share their knowledge whenever this will have a positive impact upon their daily work. It is therefore important that companies do not look upon knowledge-sharing as an extra chore but rather as part of the daily routine. The next chapter deals with this view of knowledge based on the need for collective involvement.

CHAPTER 8

THE INDIVIDUAL LEARNING TRAP

1. INTRODUCTION

Whenever we analysed the different knowledge-sharing practices by raising questions such as *"Who shares knowledge?"* or *"Whose knowledge is meant to be shared?"*, we saw that most initiatives were limited to the learning of individual employees. A similar observation was made when addressing the question *"Where is knowledge shared?"*. Managing knowledge-sharing seems to be perceived as an activity to support learning at the individual – and sometimes group – level. Seldom do organizations link knowledge management with the learning of the organization as a whole. These two questions consequently pointed to a second critical aspect of structuring knowledge-sharing. This critical aspect relates to our observation that most knowledge-sharing practices are geared towards individual learning while only very rarely is a link made with the organization as a whole. We consider it to be a stumbling block that knowledge management initiatives lack any organizational contribution. Moreover, we believe that many knowledge-sharing initiatives have the potential to make a positive contribution to learning at the organizational level. We label this risk of emphasizing knowledge-sharing between individuals without deriving any real benefit for the collective, the 'individual learning trap'.

In many cases, individuals share their knowledge with other individuals while this recycling does not result in any benefits for the organization. Through this, the practice of knowledge-sharing bears the hallmark of an individual learning process more than an organizational learning process.

We have already discussed the relationship between structured knowledge-sharing and organizational learning in Chapter 3. Knowledge-sharing can be seen as a support process for organizational learning. In order to transform individual learning into organizational learning, the collective acceptance of shared knowledge is of vital importance. During this process knowledge is collectively accepted as organizational knowledge. In a large number of the case studies that were researched there was absolutely no question of collective acceptance. The most important reason behind this absence of collective acceptance is the lack of managerial or organizational involvement in knowledge-sharing practices at the grass roots level.

Following on from our analysis of the individual learning trap in the following section, we go on to discuss a number of measures that will increase this collective involvement so that it contributes towards the learning process of the organization.

2. THE PRACTICE OF LEARNING WITHIN AND BY ORGANIZATIONS

Most of the companies that we researched limit themselves to a specific facet of learning. In Figure 13 the companies have been grouped within the framework of the different learning processes. A number of issues stand out.

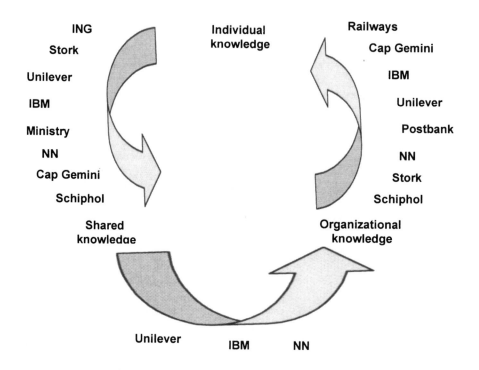

Figure 13. Companies divided according to their learning processes

Practically all the companies manage to make collective knowledge available to individual employees. For a number of companies, such as the Postbank and the Railways, this was nothing short of their main objective. At these companies the underlying reason for introducing knowledge-sharing was to improve the accessibility of the organizational knowledge that had been recorded in procedures and regulations as well as in people's heads. By gathering all this knowledge together and centralizing it in knowledge databases, the individual learning process of the employees would run more smoothly.

Figure 11 also shows that IBM, ING, Schiphol, Unilever, the Ministry of Housing, NN, and Cap Gemini consider it important to make individual knowledge available for others within the organization. In addition, Stork, Unilever, the Ministry of Housing and Cap Gemini consider it vital that individuals recycle their knowledge, so that they also provide opportunities to create new knowledge out of this knowledge exchange.

IBM, NN, and Unilever appear throughout the entire cycle. This means that these organizations support the following three learning processes:

– *Individual learning processes* by making collective knowledge accessible to individuals.

– *Individual and group learning processes* by making the knowledge of an individual accessible to another individual or groups of individuals.

– *Organizational learning processes* by making shared knowledge available to the collective.

Unilever, for example, ensures that group learning processes are supported through its workshops. Individuals are given enough latitude to exchange knowledge with one another and develop new knowledge. This new knowledge is subsequently used by the organization to implement changes. In this way, for example, an organization might learn about new marketing strategies or new products. It does this by taking the so-called communities that emanate from the workshops seriously and by listening to their new ideas (Von Krogh 1998).

A well-known example within Unilever of organizational learning based on group learning processes is the establishment of a brand new factory as a result of knowledge development within a community. The new organizational knowledge is then used once again by other employees within Unilever and by new recruits. In this way, shared knowledge is converted into collective knowledge and, in turn, further serves as input to the individual learning processes, which completes the learning cycle.

Collective acceptance of shared knowledge takes place at IBM via an editorial board made up of experts. These experts act as a kind of 'knowledge-jury'. They determine whether or not the experiences sent in by individuals are useful, relevant and interesting enough for the collective to be included in the collective knowledge database.

At NN collective acceptance occurs specifically via the experts: the knowledge coordinators, specialists and contact persons. Through their status - which was obtained mainly because of their many years' experience in processing insurance claims - the claim processors consider their knowledge to be valuable and reliable. Their role can be compared in this context to that of the specialists at IBM. Knowledge obtained through contact with the claim processors is first judged according to its suitability for collective use, after which it is disseminated. This takes place both verbally via the expert-network as well as in an electronic format.

Despite the fact that some companies are not striving towards an organization-wide impact with their knowledge practices - the Postbank and the Netherlands Railways for example - we still see various ways in which their organizational learning processes can be improved. This is certainly the case when the individual learning process results in knowledge that might also be relevant to the organization as a whole. In this way, policymakers at the Ministry of Housing would learn about the sustainable building project, employees at Stork learn about new production methods, conductors at the Netherlands Railways learn which routes need the most support and the Postbank's employees can see what customers think of the latest savings schemes. All this knowledge can be relevant for the organization as a whole too. Whenever such 'grass roots knowledge' is accepted at the organizational level, then other staff members and new recruits can subsequently learn from it.

The Sales and Customer Services department at the Postbank fails to exploit an excellent opportunity to learn from its customers. No systematic feedback about customer enquiries and problems is channelled via Customer Services through to the organization. Indeed, for an organization whose only physical contact with the customer is via the telephone, this is a missed opportunity.

There are also benefits for the Railways that remain untapped. In this case, it is not just about knowledge-sharing among the conductors, but in particular about the additional benefit that the Railways can derive through feedback from the conductor to the process manager. That information is now used in 'people management' but its potential at the organizational level remains unexploited. When monitoring the conductors it is, for example, good to be able to give an instant response to reports of aggressive behaviour. At the end of the day, however, the company will only get something out of this if the upper echelons do something with these experiences. Up until now, learning has been restricted to the individual level.

At Stork learning remains limited, in many cases, to group learning without these knowledge-sharing practices having any influence at the organizational level. The knowledge created by Stork's working groups is merely retained in reports and saved and archived at a central point. Stork only recently started to publish these reports electronically. Interest in this new knowledge has proved to be disappointing. Reports are seldom looked up and there is the usual level of scepticism regarding their use. One of the most important reasons why knowledge-sharing within Stork does not lead to organizational learning, is the absence of collective involvement, which is due to Stork's decentralized structure.

At the Ministry of Housing too, knowledge exchange via the digital discussion platforms seldom results in its organizational knowledge being fine-tuned. Through this, interactive policy development remains at the group learning level rather than the organizational learning level. An important reason for this is that the Ministry's employees often consider the knowledge-sharing and individual learning that occurs via the digital platforms to be irrelevant or superfluous. Support from upper management and an enthusiastic champion are perhaps the most important reasons why the Ministry finally decided to include the use of the discussion platforms in the companies 'communication mix' and as such treat them as a structural part of the organization.

Just as at the Ministry of Housing and Stork, support from the top at Cap Gemini is an important reason why, despite the disappointing level of use, the local intranet CapCom and the world-wide network Galaxy are still maintained. However, it still cannot be said that there is collective acceptance of the knowledge contained in the two intranets. The most important explanation for this is, perhaps, that consultants prefer to use personal networks rather than technical ones to swap experiences. We will explore this further in the next chapter.

For some of the companies that we researched, this study was premature: they are still in the process of sowing the seeds of knowledge management and are not yet ready to harvest the fruits. ING Barings, for example, has collected knowledge from different countries and has made this public with the help of its intranet. When we were carrying out our research this was still seldom used.

To conclude, we see that the knowledge-sharing cases that were studied support individual and group learning in particular, but seldom learning by the organization as a whole. The results of the knowledge-sharing practices are not considered to be relevant by others who are outside the network of the knowledge-sharing players. Companies fail to exploit opportunities to improve their organizations. The cause of this individual learning trap is the lack of collective involvement in knowledge-sharing. Knowledge-sharing is mainly looked upon as a grass roots activity for which interference at an organizational level is not necessary. Avoiding this trap requires collective involvement to be encouraged. A number of methods to achieve this are discussed below.

3. FIGHT THE LEARNING TRAP: STIMULATE COLLECTIVE INVOLVEMENT

Structured forms of knowledge-sharing are often presented using the broad term knowledge management. This often occurs in the form of projects. The initiative then requires additional effort in the short term. This type of approach towards knowledge-sharing is risky because it hardly involves the organizational level at all. The work of the individual improves and sometimes a group's work does as well, but the main body of people employed within an organization does not derive any benefit from the grass roots, knowledge-sharing practices.

The most important cause of this, in our eyes, is the lack of organization-wide involvement in knowledge-sharing. Collective involvement in the knowledge-sharing initiative is easier to achieve when a company looks upon knowledge-sharing as an intrinsic part of the way in which it operates. In this type of company, work is organized in such a way that knowledge exchange, individual learning and knowledge acquisition are stimulated rather than hampered. This may sound like an open-and-shut case, but in practice few companies fit this profile. Knowledge-sharing as a way of thinking and behaving means that knowledge-sharing is continuously taking place. During our research, we encountered a number of strategies that can increase collective acceptance.

Management's contribution
One of the causes of falling into the individual learning trap is the predominantly limited contribution from management in actually sharing their knowledge. The majority of the case studies that were researched took place between individual knowledge workers. Generally speaking, management's role has been primarily reserved to initiate or support knowledge-sharing. In practice, it appears that this is not enough. Knowledge-sharing cannot remain restricted to the operational level.

Management has a key role to play in encouraging the acceptance of shared knowledge. For example, if knowledge-sharing processes are to be collectively accepted it is important that management is fully aware of which groups share what knowledge. Should they ignore knowledge-sharing processes, then potentially valuable knowledge might be lost.

It is important for collective acceptance that management itself sets an example in sharing knowledge. It is often the case that management expresses the wish that people would share more knowledge with each other, while not doing anything in this area itself. Managers should therefore also learn to first ask themselves questions such as whether they contribute enough to knowledge-sharing, with whom they share knowledge, when they share it and, in particular, when and why they do *not* share knowledge. This type of personal reflection gives an insight into the reasons why others share knowledge or indeed why they shrink away from it.

Formal knowledge-sharing functions
It is often assumed that formal knowledge-sharing functions create involvement on an organization-wide level. Practice shows, however, that it would be prudent to exercise caution with regard to such expectations.

There is much confusion surrounding the newly launched knowledge management functions. Over the past years discussions have centred around the profile of the Chief Knowledge Officer (e.g. Earl and Scott 1999; Davenport and Prusak 1998). People have been appointed to this position without a profile being drawn up beforehand. The Chief Knowledge Officer can, for example, be someone who is responsible for the information and documentation department within a large company. Other companies retain the term 'knowledge manager' for this position.

In conjunction with the formal roles within a company, an area of tension has arisen between knowledge-sharing and hierarchical responsibility. This is certainly the case when participation in a formal or informal role such as, for example, knowledge manager or 'stimulator' is at the expense of functional responsibility. This type of tension exists, for example, at Unilever, NN and Stork.

Certainly at companies where a strongly decentralized structure is in place, we see that participation in knowledge-sharing processes results in people shying away from their operational responsibility. Because they have less time available to carry out their operational tasks, tensions can arise between the employee and his or her immediate superior. This is often exacerbated because it is not immediately clear how one's own department can benefit by taking part in a 'corporate' knowledge network. The problem is not actually any different than that of supervising people in matrix organizations. What is important is that management at different levels within the company are aware of this problem. Whenever it is a matter of organization-wide involvement, it is assumed that this area of tension will be less problematic.

Another disadvantage of specific knowledge-sharing positions is that these suggest that someone has the final responsibility for knowledge as an organizational resource. In view of the fact that knowledge permeates every aspect of an organization, this is a dangerous assumption. If only a small group of people is responsible for supporting and stimulating knowledge-sharing, then this will easily lead to individual responsibility being hedged.

Judging from what we see in practice, it seems to be wise to be cautious - at least for the time being - about creating new positions. If knowledge-sharing is part of the day-to-day functioning of an organization, then everyone is a knowledge worker and each individual is responsible for the way in which knowledge is handled.

Support from top management
Different reasons can be given why support from top management can make a positive contribution (Drew 1998). Support is, for example, necessary to drive through the message that knowledge-sharing is very important for the company. In addition, support is necessary when the knowledge-sharing initiative requires financial support or a change in infrastructure. Of course, the same applies to facilitating the necessary changes within the organization.

Common to all companies was that people cited support from top management as an important factor when creating involvement at the organization-wide level. At the companies that we analysed, it is certain that without the support of top management the knowledge-sharing initiatives would not have been successful (Unilever) or would not have been implemented (Stork).

The formal termination of the knowledge management project at Schiphol also highlights the importance of this factor. A change of course as a result of the appointment of a new President-Director had repercussions for the development of products and services. Schiphol now focuses mainly on 'operational excellence' in its treatment of passengers, luggage and freight. According to the top management, the knowledge activities of the knowledge centre that are geared towards the professional employee could not be reconciled with this philosophy.

At the same time, support from top management also makes the practice of sharing knowledge extremely complex. Knowledge-sharing is essential for an organization, but employees frequently experience the deliberate initiation by management as threatening. Knowledge management from the top down contains irrevocable risks.

Measuring knowledge
Support from top management requires the results of knowledge-sharing to be transparent. At this point, we enter into the debate on whether knowledge and knowledge-sharing can be measured. A frequently heard viewpoint is that knowledge management projects are doomed to fail because nobody can judge whether they are successful or not. In the absence of good yardsticks, companies invent solutions such as measuring the reuse of knowledge. IBM has developed a tool to measure the value of knowledge. At Cap Gemini the formal position is that the management of knowledge must be linked to formal objectives and formal criteria. Unilever has much more of a deep-rooted conviction that knowledge-sharing deserves attention. The company sees the effects in practice without being able to attach hard financial figures to them.

One reason why measuring knowledge-sharing initiatives is popular, is the fact that knowledge management is launched in the form of projects. To keep projects manageable, concrete goals are required with measurable results. Knowledge management projects have to demonstrate the project's value for the organization.

The need to measure often results in the wrong measurement being emphasized: the number of people who used the intranet or the amount of documents that were submitted or consulted. These measures lead to an emphasis on the stock approach to knowledge, downplaying the flow approach.

As with the creation of new responsibilities, it would also seem that caution is the best policy with regard to measuring knowledge. This applies in particular when organizations recognize the importance of knowledge-sharing as routine and bring it into practice. Measuring knowledge might involve top management and share holders more in the knowledge initiative, but in the long term measuring can be lethal for the initiative (Davenport and Prusak 1998). Measuring knowledge and knowledge-sharing is difficult and maybe even impossible, but that does not go to say that because of this knowledge-sharing does not deserve to be stimulated.

4. SUMMARY

Knowledge-sharing cannot be a goal in itself. The results of knowledge-sharing ought to be publicly or collectively accepted so as to support the primary process of the knowledge workers in turn. When this is not the case, the organization as a whole cannot derive any benefit from the structured knowledge-sharing. The emphasis therefore lies at the level of individual and group learning and not on organizational learning as a whole. In several practical case studies in this book knowledge continues to be shared between individuals and never rises above this level. The most important reason for this individual learning trap is the lack of collective involvement in local knowledge-sharing practices.

Different measures to stimulate involvement are possible, such as actively involving management in knowledge-sharing, and support from top management. Examples of this are the creation of new positions and measuring knowledge, the latter of which is also meant to involve top management and the shareholders in the initiative. In practice, it appears that these two last approaches do not always result in an increased collective acceptance of knowledge. In chapter 10 we use the concept of social capital to discuss in more detail how collective involvement can be stimulated in the future.

CHAPTER 9

THE ICT TRAP

1. INTRODUCTION

Whenever we ask the question *'How is knowledge is shared?'* there appears to be a consensus of opinion among all companies that knowledge is shared with the help of ICT. What are generally meant in this context are systems to record knowledge.

We can hereby simultaneously answer the question 'W*hich knowledge is shared?'*. The answer is that organizations tend to bias towards managing codified knowledge. By stressing explicit or codified knowledge one can speak of a stock approach toward knowledge sharing. The flow-approach receives less attention, or at least less formal attention.

Emphasizing ICT as a support for knowledge-sharing as well as stressing a stock-approach are the direct results of an ICT-driven approach to knowledge-sharing. Organizations that are preoccupied with structured forms of knowledge-sharing should be wary of falling into the ICT trap. This trap boils down to companies being inclined to initiate knowledge-sharing (or knowledge management) with a bias towards technology. In that case, insufficient consideration is given to the support requirements of specific knowledge-sharing procedures and learning processes. When we talk about the ICT trap we are in no way rejecting the use of ICT to support knowledge-sharing. However, we are exploring the dangers of a one-sided, ICT-driven approach. In section 9.3 we show how the ICT trap can be avoided.

2. ICT DETERMINISM

Table 9 gives an overview of the number of articles on knowledge management that have appeared in reputable international scientific journals. The analysis focussed on the frequency with which an article on knowledge management explicitly referred to other thematic categories (by means of keywords) (Scarbrough and Swan 2001).

Table 9. Publications on knowledge management in reputable international scientific journals.

KM related themes	Number of publications	Percentage
Information technology	73	40
Information systems	51	28
Strategic management	35	19
Human Resource Management	9	5
Other ('Consultancy', libraries, accounting, marketing, academic)	16	8
Total	184	100

Source: Scarborough and Swan (2001)

The table shows that the focus on ICT dominates the literature on knowledge management. This dominance does not only indicate a scientific interest. Many knowledge management projects have their origins in the ICT world. With the rise of advanced technology, opportunities to facilitate knowledge-sharing within organizations are on the increase. Lately such an ICT-oriented approach has received more criticism. Science and consultancy both embrace the view that if the emphasis is placed on ICT then this will represent a threat to knowledge-sharing. At the same time, there is an overall consensus that ICT can fulfil an important role here. Certainly in practice, most knowledge management initiatives are (still) ICT-driven[13].

In theory, an ICT-driven approach need not necessarily be a trap. There could be situations where the organization as a whole benefits from the potential afforded by ICT in supporting and initiating knowledge-sharing. One good example of this is the RailPocket device used at Dutch Railways. The trap lurks particularly in the assumption that ICT can positively support and improve knowledge-sharing. This assumption often results in the wrong combination of, on the one hand, the need for support for knowledge-sharing processes and, on the other, the use of ICT applications.

Too heavy a bias towards ICT manifests itself in the following three myths (see also Swan et al 1998):

−   New technological opportunities improve organizations.

−   Everyone is capable of using ICT applications.

−   Knowledge can be stored in systems.

We will discuss these myths below with special attention to the last mentioned myth.

Technological potential leads to organizational improvement
Technological determinism considers technology to be the driving force behind progress. Many initiatives for innovations are based on the idea that the way in which people, organizations and society function can be improved by introducing some new form of technology. This type of technology-driven approach can also be found in many of the knowledge-sharing initiatives discussed in part two of this book. In this way, the introduction of intranets at Cap Gemini and ING Barings were inspired by the idea that technology would lead to improvement. The introduction of discussion groups by the Ministry of Housing was also motivated by a conviction in the potential of technology. When we come to analyse the results of all of this, we should at the very least question this so-called improvement bias (Huysman 2000). Clearly, it is not the technology itself but the way people use it that determines whether progress is made.

Everyone is capable of using ICT applications
Another manifestation of ICT determinism is the assumption that people can get to grips with technology. In Chapter 7 we discussed the fact that management implicitly believes that people are prepared to contribute to knowledge-sharing. And yet nobody asks the question *'Why should they do this?'*

Alongside the question of how great is the need, the question of competence is frequently ignored. A danger when implementing technology is that the ICT application goes beyond the ability of those having to use it. ICT-driven initiatives run the risk that the organization will not have the capacity to live up to the demands that the technology makes upon it. This is why civil servants at the Ministry of Housing had difficulties with the digital discussion platforms as they were not used to working with this type of communication. Many civil servants had no experience with Internet use and some even did not have access to the net from their office. Consequently, civil servants hardly participated in the digital discussions at all.

The use of ICT applications such as Lotus Notes sometimes requires a lengthy learning period. This can be quite discouraging, which results in it being used less and less. In essence, it concerns old lessons on the use of ICT-technology that come to the fore when knowledge is shared via an intranet. The management and quality of information that can be found on an intranet is therefore very important (Choo et al 2000).

All knowledge can be stored in systems
A popular view in the knowledge management literature - as well as in the cases researched by us - is that knowledge can be housed in technical systems. Echoes from the legacy of the information-management era resound here.

It is impossible to store all forms of knowledge in a system. The knowledge that can be stored in systems always consists of explicit knowledge; knowledge that can be saved and passed on via books, reports and intranets. When knowledge is saved in a system it becomes transformed into explicit, codified knowledge (Zack 1999).

Explicit and tacit dimensions of knowledge

We use Polanyi's (1966) assumption that all knowledge has a tacit dimension and that knowledge exists on a spectrum. "At one extreme it is almost completely tacit, that is, semiconscious and unconscious knowledge held in peoples' head and bodies. At the other end of the spectrum, knowledge is almost completely explicit, or codified, structured, and accessible to people other than the individuals originating it. Most knowledge, of course, exists in between the extremes." (Leonard and Sensiper 1998)

A lot of knowledge is implicit by nature and appears to be difficult to share with others, let alone store in a system. In the case of implicit knowledge, the human being is both the knowledge carrier and the vehicle through with the knowledge is passed on. A huge drawback with implicit knowledge is that people are often incapable of transferring the knowledge. In most cases, implicit knowledge is transferred by making knowledge explicit. Hedlund (1994) calls this process of transforming the implicit into explicit 'Articulation'; Nonaka and Takeuchi (1995) refer to it as 'externalization'.

In order to support the sharing of explicit and tacit knowledge, Zack (1999) makes a distinction between integrative applications and interactive applications.

Integrative applications exhibit a sequential flow of explicit knowledge into and out of the repository. Consumers (readers) and producers (authors) of knowledge interact with one another through the repository rather than directly. Zack argues that the applications vary in the extent to which users and producers are members of the same community. He labels applications 'electronic publishing' in case consumers and producers do not belong to the same community. In that case, the content remains stable when published while the original author makes possible updates. An example is the publication of a periodic newsletter on the intranet or the Railways mobile knowledge base.

"Integrated knowledge-bases' on the other hand are applications that are used by consumers and producers who are members of the same community. The repository provides a means to integrate and build on collective knowledge. Examples are the best practices databases were practices are collected, integrated and shared among people confronted with similar problems, such as Cap Com.

"Interactive applications" are focused on supporting interaction among people holding tacit knowledge. In this case the repository is a by-product of interaction and collaboration, rather than the primary focus. Zack (1999) makes a distinction based on the level of expertise between producers and consumers and the degree of structure imposed on their interaction. He refers to applications that are used between expert and novice and structured around a discrete problem or plan, as 'distributed learning applications'. The knowledge base of NN provides an example of such an application.

"Forums" are applications that in contrast to distributed learning applications are used to support interaction among those performing common practices that tend to be more *ad hoc* or emergent. The discussion platforms of the Ministry of Housing provide a good example of such forums.

Even though there are methods to convert implicit knowledge to explicit knowledge, such as 'mind-mapping' techniques as was the case with the Postbank, extracting the knowledge from the knowledge carrier can still be problem. In Chapter 7 we have already discussed the implications for sharing meta-knowledge. Meta-knowledge cannot be recorded in technical networks and requires the support of social personal networks. In that case, tacit knowledge does not need to be transformed into explicit knowledge in order to share it with others. While technical applications are usually not very effective tools to support tacit knowledge-sharing, social networks seem to be well suited for knowledge-sharing. What is needed is the support of social networks and knowledge connections to enable transfer (Boland and Tenkasi 1995, Von Krogh 1998, Leonard 1998, Prusak 1997)

Our research provides examples that illustrate how employees would rather make use of social personal networks than be dependent upon electronic ones. Despite the fact that knowledge-sharing is common through the stock-approach, employees apparently prefer to make use of a flow approach towards knowledge-sharing. This observation might relate back to Polyani's (1966) argument that all knowledge has a tacit dimension.

Cap Gemini employees make particular use of the reference function in their CapCom system. Whenever somebody wants more information about, for example, a certain client, staff uses CapCom to look up the individual whom they want to contact. This reference system simplifies the internal networks within Cap Gemini and thereby supports knowledge-sharing according to the flow-approach.

NN also uses the knowledge database system, and the search function in particular. In the event of more detailed information being required about, for example, a special claim for damages, employees quickly abandon their knowledge databases and approach a senior staff member, more often than not because this is a lot quicker. Each claim often has some specific ingredient that deviates from the standard routines, so the knowledge recorded in the knowledge database is unable to provide a solution.

Furthermore, knowledge database systems can never be 100 percent up-to-date as they cannot record an (emotional) state of mind. Next to speed, this is another important reason why the social network is preferred to the electronic network, as the specialists can tell you how you should behave with a particular client. Social interactions offer more for such questions than the use of explicit, context-based knowledge.

Unilever learned its lesson in this context. A number of years ago, Unilever began workshops with 'knowledge mapping', the main objective of which was to record the shared knowledge in knowledge databases. These knowledge databases involve content and procedural knowledge on products; for example, detailed knowledge on manufacturing tomato sauces. This knowledge database provides support to the primary process world-wide. In practice, it seems that articulating knowledge in a knowledge database is perceived as being less important than the personal knowledge-sharing that existed both during and after the workshop. Unilever subsequently relegated ICT to the background in its workshops. In addition, the company switched from a stock-approach to a flow-approach.

3. AVOID THE ICT TRAP: PREVENT ICT DETERMINISM

The ICT trap lurks in the dangerous assumption that all relevant knowledge can be recorded in systems, that ICT is an instrument to improve knowledge-sharing and that people have the skills to work with technology. There are several measures that can be taken to avoid falling into the ICT trap.

An integral approach towards knowledge-sharing
It is extremely important that the issue of managing knowledge-sharing receives a multidisciplinary approach. Initiatives for structured knowledge-sharing at many companies originate from the ICT-management team. At the same time, many companies already have an image about the importance of a multidisciplinary approach based on previous reorganization schemes or on the basis of implementing ICT. Consider the rule of thumb that says that technical changes only demand 20% of a company's attention, while changing people requires 80% of a company's attention. Although the recalcitrance of 'soft factors' is generally known, there is still a great temptation to begin with the technology because fewer problems are expected there.

The complexity of stimulating knowledge-sharing - certainly with the use of ICT - demands an effort in which different functional departments throughout the organization must be involved. In knowledge-sharing programmes such as those at Unilever and IBM we see that a multidisciplinary approach is an explicit point of view, but that the knowledge of the organizational or human aspects is not well represented within the support group.

Knowledge-sharing initiatives are more successful when both a technical infrastructure is present as well as a well-established social network and if an adequate organizational structure has been developed. We see, for example, at the knowledge storage project at NN, a synergetic relationship evolving between the technical side and the social personal network.

The danger of an integral approach is that companies might opt for a blueprint model in which the entire knowledge architecture is mapped out beforehand. The implementation of knowledge architecture then reduces flexibility, while this is important to stimulate knowledge-sharing. With an integral approach, companies concentrate better on improving the activities that they already carry out. Here, the most successful seem to be the initiatives - such as the knowledge networks and the communities - that focus on a specific problem area.

Matching ICT with knowledge-sharing requirements
ICT is often introduced with the idea that it will stimulate knowledge-sharing and make it easier. In this scenario, insufficient attention is given to the need for technical support that a specific type of knowledge-sharing calls for. In order to avoid the dangers inherent in too strong an ICT-determinism, it is important for the organization to be aware of the need for knowledge-sharing and the specific demands that this need entails. In an ideal situation, the role of ICT should preferably be derived from the need for knowledge and knowledge-sharing and not the other way around.

Figure 14 gives an ideal typical role model of the process through which knowledge-sharing initiatives take place and the role of ICT support.

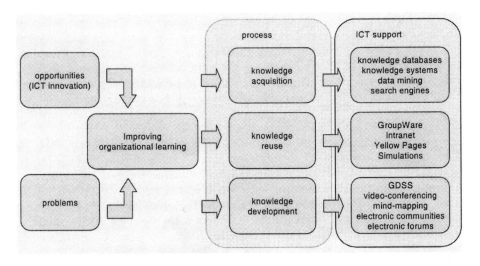

Figure 14. The role of ICT in the introduction of a knowledge-sharing initiative.

Depending on the needs of the organization, knowledge-sharing - and with this ICT support - can take different forms:

ICT and knowledge acquisition
Whenever individuals acquire knowledge from the organization, this is often explicit knowledge. At NN for example, the knowledge built up over years by the organization concerning how claims are processed, has been recorded in a knowledge database system. The same applies to the knowledge about savings schemes at the Postbank. Knowledge that was previously tied up with individuals has, over the years, assumed a collective character and has been disconnected from its original individual carrier. Because this collective knowledge is explicit and independent of a particular context, it lends itself well to a stock approach towards knowledge and can therefore be made accessible via a knowledge database system.

ICT and knowledge reuse
Whenever there is a need for knowledge to be exchanged between individuals and whenever this knowledge is not implicit by nature, intranets offer support. Here a number of peripheral conditions apply. The information must be up-to-date, information overload should be avoided and the information should be useful. In addition, it is advisable to introduce intranets in stages: begin with simple but extremely useful information and in this way ensure that a critical mass of users exists.

Also, intranets should not be treat as substitutes for social networks. On the contrary, our research showed that intranets are often used in combination with social networks and frequently strengthen them. It is therefore important to pay just as much attention to the social-organizational aspects as to the technical aspects.

The need to take the social embeddedness of intranets into serious account, is one of the main causes of intranet failure, and requires careful analysis of various information levels of the organization: the infrastructure, infostructure and info culture (Choo et al 2000). The latter dimension in particular is often ignored and requires in-depth analysis of the organizational norms, values and routines regarding knowledge sharing.

ICT and knowledge development
Knowledge development requires different support again than that which can be provided through a knowledge database system or via an intranet. The creation of knowledge calls for direct human intervention and interaction (Faye and Prusak 1998; Leonard and Sensiper 1998). Despite the promising noises made about the potential of advanced ICT applications, ICT does not possess the wealth of human interaction, not even with advanced GroupWare systems. In practice we still see few advanced forms of ICT geared towards knowledge development. In those instances where the emphasis was upon knowledge creation the contribution from ICT was

relegated to the background. Out of the GroupWare applications, only Lotus Notes seems to be accepted on a wide scale.

The technological path of the organization
Each company has its own experiences that influence the way in which innovations are introduced as well as their potential (Nelson and Winter 1982, Rosenberg and Frischtak 1985). This not only determines the infrastructure within which people work, but also certain preferences for suppliers and ICT-support. In addition, these experiences also influence the organization's ability to change.

For the sake of convenience, we often talk about an ICT-friendly or an ICT-hostile culture. In fact it is often peoples' personal experiences that lie at the root of the factors that influence the ability to adapt. Continuous changes in applications tend to alienate people if they always have to learn new things for the sake of the organizational well-being.

A company's 'ability to absorb' also resides in collective experiences (Cohen and Levinthal 1991). The ease with which previous ICT-related change processes have evolved, or the very problems that these brought, often determines the company's attitude. When the wrong type of introduction is chosen - for example, a convoluted intranet with all the trimmings - the organization has to make a supreme effort to galvanize people into using it.

4. SUMMARY

In this chapter we discussed the ICT trap. With this we mean the danger of placing too much faith in ICT's ability to improve knowledge-sharing. Whenever we ask the questions *'How is knowledge shared?"* and *"Which knowledge does this involve?"* we notice that ICT often plays a dominant role in supporting the sharing of explicit knowledge. This technical bias was not only apparent in the companies that we researched, indeed ICT is almost inextricably bound up with knowledge-sharing in the literature, but even more so in knowledge management practices. Although the role of ICT in knowledge-sharing should certainly not be underestimated, in practice an integral approach is more successful than a more technical one. In addition, organizations would be better advised to treat ICT more as a by-product of knowledge-sharing than the other way around. Even if management is convinced that ICT is important for knowledge-sharing, employees regularly avoid using the technology. In practice, ICT's role seems limited while social personal networks are more important for knowledge-sharing. This is because, among other things, most if not all knowledge has a tacit dimension while the need for meta-knowledge remains. The role of ICT in this should be more about connecting people and not so much about acquiring and disseminating knowledge.

CHAPTER 10

EPILOGUE

1. INTRODUCTION

So far, we have reached the conclusion that sharing knowledge is a collective rather than an individual activity, that it will only occur naturally in situations where individuals benefit from sharing and that ICT can only support it, not replace it. We showed how managing knowledge-sharing cannot rely solely on knowledge management tools, nor on reward structures, formal knowledge management strategies, chief knowledge officers, training programmes, etc. We rounded up this discussion rather negatively with some critical observations about the downside of knowledge management. Nevertheless, this should not imply that we do not see a future for the management of knowledge-sharing. On the contrary, there are various reasons why managing knowledge-sharing is extremely important. In fact, we are so convinced of the importance of knowledge management that we believe organizations should strive to make it a routine part of their daily activities.

Knowledge-sharing has become a key concern to organizations, not only because of the growing importance of the value of knowledge work, but also because of the increasing speed at which changes take place. Changing organizational boundaries and identities as well as the growth of virtual organizations, e-lancers[14], teleworkers, and geographically dispersed teams, increases the difficulty of monitoring and controlling knowledge. It is hard to find, hard to move when you want it to and also hard to move when you don't want it to (Brown and Duguid 2000a). Both in spite of and because of these difficulties, organizations, especially large ones, try hard to manage knowledge. This urge to get a grip on knowledge and to leverage it to create competitive advantage is understandable and constitutes an important topic for discussion among organizational practitioners and theorists alike. However, the currently accepted or most generally discussed and practiced way of coping with knowledge meets with resistance at various levels.

In this book, we discussed the three traps into which organizations tend to fall when engaging in knowledge management initiatives. The traps relate to the tendency of organizations to concentrate too much on:

- the role of ICT in facilitating knowledge-sharing;
- individual learning as the purpose of knowledge-sharing; and,
- imposing managerial needs upon knowledge-sharing.

In the last section of this book we will bring together the various recommendations to support knowledge-sharing as discussed throughout part three of this book and present them as management recommendations. These recommendations are all concerned with coping with managerial dilemmas: how to ensure that people share knowledge and that the organization benefits from it, without having to enforce it. These recommendations build on a view of knowledge management that we see as being the second wave of knowledge management. There are some signals that this next generation is already on its way[15] as several authors already approach knowledge-sharing as if it were inextricably bound up with the daily practices of organizing (e.g. Brown and Duguid 2000b, Davenport and Prusak 1998, Von Krogh et al 2000, Wenger 1998). Before discussing ways to manage knowledge in this next generation, we will first give a normative description of what we mean by this next phase of knowledge management and on what principles it is based.

2. TOWARDS THE SECOND WAVE OF KNOWLEDGE MANAGEMENT

Table 10 provides an overview of the main differences between the first and second wave of developments in the area of knowledge management.

Table 10. Differences between the first and second waves of knowledge management

Research question	1st wave	2nd wave
Why is knowledge shared?	Managerial needs	Part of daily work: as a routine
When is knowledge shared?	When there is an opportunity to do so	When there is a need to do so
Where is knowledge shared?	Operational level	Organization-wide
Whose knowledge is managed?	Individual: human capital	Collective: social capital
What knowledge is shared?	Codified	Tacit and Codified
How is knowledge shared?	Repository systems and electronic networks.	Via personal and electronic networks

Below we will discuss these differences by addressing the following important characteristics of the second wave of knowledge management:

— Knowledge-sharing as a routine

— Care in managing knowledge-sharing

— Social capital and Communities of Practice

–   Objectifying local knowledge

–   New role of ICT

2.1   Knowledge-sharing as a routine

The three traps discussed in this book cannot be solved until knowledge management stops being looked at as an out-of-the-ordinary, supplementary organizational phenomenon. We have seen that most organizations have a tendency to explicitly manage and be in control of knowledge. This is understandable, as many new phenomena first require explicit investment before they become routine. This was, for example, the case with quality management. But over time, knowledge-sharing should become an inherent part of the day-to-day activities within an organization. People will not share knowledge if it requires additional attention, especially when it does not contribute directly to their daily work. Or as Davenport and Prusak (1998, p. 164) put it:

> "(ultimately) knowledge management work needs to be blended in with all other activities in the organization or it's unlikely to be effective".

Quality movement as an exemplar
Botkin (1999) as well as Brown and Duguid (2000) compare knowledge management with the discussions surrounding the quality movement in the late eighties, beginning of the nineties. Botkin thereby argues that just like quality, knowledge-sharing also affects every part of the organization. Also, in the same way that quality does, managing knowledge-sharing will provide competitive advantage in the beginning but, as everyone will adopt it, managing knowledge will become a requirement for staying in business. Moreover, like quality, managing knowledge requires investment before it becomes routine.

The challenge that many organizations face is working out how to turn this explicit attention into implicit attention. If an organization fails to make knowledge-sharing a routine part of its day-to-day operations, it might lose the competitive edge that it once held by initiating knowledge management projects (Botkin 1999). Furthermore, if organizations fail to institutionalize knowledge-sharing, then knowledge management initiatives will only last for as long as the knowledge management champion and his or her initiatives continue to be accepted and financially supported. As our analysis of the obstacles to knowledge management in part three revealed, this could well be for a pretty brief spell.

Most of the past and present knowledge management literature and especially knowledge management practices relate to the first knowledge management wave in which knowledge-sharing and consequently learning is seen as being in addition to the work processes within the organization. The first wave sees knowledge management as an organizational phenomenon that needs investment and explicit attention. Given the enormous growth of knowledge management ideas, tools, books, gurus, and especially practices, we can now say that it has gained this attention. In fact, this first wave is now facing growing criticism now that it is starting to bounce up against a wall of resistance. It is ready to be succeeded by a second wave that provides the necessary conditions for institutionalizing knowledge management. With the second wave the focus is directed towards the conditions that stimulate knowledge-sharing as a routine.

One important reason why the first wave of knowledge management initiatives increasingly met with resistance is that knowledge-sharing cannot be forced; people will only share knowledge if there is a personal reason to do so. As knowledge owners, people have the power to decide if, when, how, and with whom they will share knowledge. It is an illusion to think that these decisions can be forced upon individuals. It is only when organizations acknowledge this, that the next step in the evolution of knowledge management can be made. In the second wave of knowledge management it will be the practitioners themselves who manage their own knowledge as they are in the best position to do so. In the words of Botkin (1999, p.102);

> "The large corporate goal is to develop large numbers of people who are self-organizing, self-managing and self-guided in creating their own flow of learning and stock of knowledge".

Taking the power of individuals in deciding to contribute to knowledge-sharing seriously means that organizational conditions must be changed in such a way that people would like to share. Fortunately, these changing conditions do not always require different organizational structures, reward systems, positions, etc. In fact, we observed that people often do feel the need to learn and share knowledge with others in situations where this would help them do their work better, more efficiently and with more satisfaction. This certainly applies to situations in which knowledge-sharing contributes to the daily operations of the organization. All cases dealing with ICT tools to support knowledge retrieval as discussed in chapter 4, were successful in the sense that they formed an integral part of the daily practices. That they were successful has much to do with the fact that the tools contributed to people's work. Although in some cases extra effort was required, this was outweighed by the benefits of work improvement.

Likewise, in the knowledge exchange cases discussed in Chapter 5 we also saw that people rely heavily on others in order to learn and to perform their jobs more effectively. Remarkably, the fact that learning and knowledge-sharing is part of people's daily operations has often not been taken seriously by management (Brown and Duguid 1991; Wenger 1998). With respect to the claim processors at NN for example, sharing knowledge with others would improve their daily practices.

Without asking for advice or providing information to others, the claim processor would become isolated and be perceived as being of little use to the rest of the community. At first, NN management failed to take these informal learning processes seriously or realize how important they were and the benefits that they could bring. Instead, they introduced knowledge databases to replace the knowledge that was shared among claim processors so as to avoid too much interdependency between people. Paradoxically, interdependency turned out to be one of the important factors for success for the claim processors at NN. Over time, management realized the importance of personal networks and has now provided the organizational conditions needed to support these networks. The knowledge base now has much more of a supporting role rather than a dominant one with regard to NN's knowledge management.

Something similar happened at Cap Gemini. While top management was busy talking about the need to introduce knowledge management and the need to use Cap Com and Galaxy to share knowledge, a continuous process of knowledge-sharing among consultants was already taking place behind the scenes. Here again, these informal or non-canonical practices (Brown and Duguid 1991) were not taken seriously by Cap Gemini's management so the organization could not learn from it. Obviously, the fact that people nonetheless continued sharing knowledge shows that when sharing knowledge contributes to personal needs – in this case the need for professionalism - it does not require formal organizational intervention.

2.2   Care in managing knowledge-sharing

People do want to share knowledge but only if there are good reasons to do so. Personal triggers to share knowledge are, for example, when it provides recognition from significant others, when it contributes to daily practices, or when it contributes to individual learning processes. The most important obstacle to managing knowledge is management itself. The role of managers in the next generation of knowledge management will be much more on the periphery, providing opportunities for people to exchange knowledge.

It is increasingly argued that organizations should adopt a 'caring' attitude toward knowledge-sharing (Botkin, 104). Caring is gradually becoming accepted as a management verb (Botkin 1999, Ciborra 1996, Cohen and Prusak 2000, Von Krogh 1998). Caring about learning, making connections, and teaching others means that knowledge-sharing is taken seriously, that the organization learns from it and that people are inspired not only to learn individually but also to help others learn, including their own organization.

Managers as farmers
The analogy of farmers might be fruitful in relation to the new role of managers in the second stage of knowledge management. Like farming, careful management requires careful observation. Farmers

take the time to watch their cattle graze or crops grow. Everything that they have learned thanks to their past experience has made them adept in pattern recognition. This form of slow learning enables them to decide whether or not it is time to intervene. Care in management also requires a lot of monitoring from the sidelines.

Care is also required to support connections between people. Connecting people can be supported by designing and creating attractive physical encounters (Holtham and Ward, 2000). Next to physical encounters, connecting people also calls for communication technology that supports the exchange of knowledge. However, we should not fall into the well-known trap of assuming that it is technology (whether based on bricks and mortar or electronic networks) that stimulates people to communicate and share knowledge. What first needs to be addressed is the question of how to stimulate a need to share knowledge among a group of people. It is only when this need is satisfied, that physical or electronic spaces are used for knowledge-sharing purposes. The second stage in the development of knowledge management places this need for knowledge connections centre stage. For this purpose, authors within the area of organization and management increasingly start to link the idea of social capital with knowledge management (e.g. Cohen and Prusak 2000, Lesser, 2000, Nahapiet and Ghosal 1998).

2.3   Social capital and Communities of Practice

The notion of 'social capital' should be seen as an additional ingredient to the already well-known economic conditions or elements that make up organizational capital: physical capital, financial capital, and human capital. Where human capital refers to individual ability (Becker 1964), social capital refers to social networks that create opportunities. While the notion of human capital formed the core knowledge of the first wave of knowledge management, social capital can be seen as the core ingredient of the second wave of knowledge management. Together, human and social capital make up the intellectual capital of the organization. Human capital relates to individual learning but does not necessarily contribute to organizational learning. It is argued that social capital provides the conditions that nurture a willingness among these intellectual humans to connect.

Many, predominantly social constructivist organizational theorists, have pointed to the importance of social relationships as the key to organizing practices (e.g. Gergen 1994, Hosking and Morley 1991, Weick 1979). This does not only relate to organizational internal functioning. For example, Hakansan and Johansson (2001) argue that business-to-business cooperations should be analysed as being close social relationships in which the history of the relationship enforces the connection

Investing in social capital means that long term benefits such as social networks based on reciprocity, trust, and mutual respect and appreciation will last much longer than engineered networks such as organizational teams (Goshal and Nahapiet

1998). Goshal and Nahapiet (1998) argue that social capital has three dimensions that are highly interrelated and difficult to segregate in practice:

- a **structural dimension** such as network ties, network configurations and appropriable organization (e.g. Burt 1992, Coleman 1988, Granovetter 1992);

- a **cognitive dimension** such as shared codes and language, and shared narratives (e.g. Cicourel 1973, Orr 1990); and ,

- a **relational dimension** such as mutual trust, norms, obligations and identification (e.g. Cohen and Prusak 2001, Fukijama 1995).

What makes the search for its ingredients even more difficult is that social capital, like other forms of capital, accumulates when used productively (Fountain 1997).

> "For example, a group of scientists who have collaborated on a relatively small scientific project may then use their collaborative ability to propose and to complete larger, riskier research projects. They may then further use their network to address the economic revitalization of their community. Their originally small network may be extended to members of the political and business community: small cooperative ventures may grow into more ambitious undertakings as parties learn how to collaborate productively and develop reputations for trustworthiness. "

The concept of social capital in the field of knowledge-sharing is too new to provide solid empirical and statistical evidence. For example, Cohen and Prusak (2000) talk about organizations that can be "high or low on social capital" and provide stories about such organizations. A lot needs to be done in order for the concept to become more accepted both in practice as well as in academia. One of the promising ways to give the concept more credibility is to connect it with social network studies and analyses (e.g. Hanson 1999, Krackhardt 1992).

Lacking social capital at the World Cup
Investing in and harvesting social capital is extremely difficult. Look, for example, at world championships in team sports such as soccer. These organizations are very successful in investing in the three economic organizational assets: physical capital, financial capital and human capital. For the exclusive event of the world champions, teams are composed of individual top players hired for the occasion to become a new temporary team player. In the past, many national teams had the experience that although the coach of such occasional teams might be able to hire the very best, their lack of social capital might be a crucial missing ingredient to reach the top.

Likewise, not much research is done on exactly *how* to invest in social capital so that learning becomes an integral part of organizational activities. Most 'new wave' authors argue that investing in social capital implies a more important role for communities of practice[16]. According to these authors, communities and social networks are seen as the prime source of a sense of membership and commitment, the source of mutuality and trust and the places in organizations where people feel most at home and most responsible for one another. Many 'new wave' authors agree that in communities, people not only invest in their own learning but also in the learning of others. They are the main places where knowledge develops. The driving forces within communities and the key conditions that help communities stay active are mutual trust, a sense of mutuality and recognition by peers (Lesser 1999).

The effectiveness of communities
Lesser (1999) provides the following list of ways for managers to foster the effectiveness of communities: Leadership can promote importance through:
- acknowledging community activities e.g. in public forums,
taking part in communities,
- contributing to the community knowledge base,
- allocating resources (time, money, infrastructure) to support the community mission,
- sending out the message that communities are a valued part of the organizational strategy,
- using knowledge brokers who identify individuals with expertise within the community,
- hosting and facilitating on-line discussion groups,
- filtering knowledge from the outside world that members of the community would find valuable.

Most of the learning that takes place in organizations occurs informally in communities of practice (Lesser 1999). As mentioned in Chapter two, contributing to organizational learning requires three processes: internalizing organizational knowledge resulting in (re)constructed individual knowledge; externalizing individual knowledge resulting in (re)constructed shared knowledge; objectifying shared knowledge resulting in (re)constructed organizational knowledge. In this book, we have argued that these processes can be supported by various knowledge-sharing processes: internalization by knowledge gathering and externalization by knowledge exchange (for the purpose of reuse or for the purpose of knowledge creation). Objectification also takes place via these knowledge-sharing processes but occurs at a much slower pace.

It would appear that communities are organizing structures that support these various aspects of knowledge-sharing. For example, *internalizing collective knowledge* at communities of practice was originally seen as its key objective. Lave and Wenger (1990), the parents of the notion of communities of practice, introduced it to refer to communities of practice as being informal social structures that offer newcomers apprenticeship through legitimate peripheral participation. In the management and business administration literature, this meaning of the concept has not been widely adopted. In fact, the concept has become more and more popular within the field of knowledge management where it is mainly used as a knowledge management tool to support the *externalization of knowledge*, both for reuse as well as for innovation purposes. Exchanging knowledge in order to help each other and to create new knowledge is central in communities of practice. Communities of practice also provide the leverage for *objectification of shared knowledge* or the transformation of shared knowledge into collectively accepted knowledge, or organizational knowledge. As mentioned earlier, objectifying knowledge is the bridge between local learning and collective or organizational learning. Without a collective acceptance of shared knowledge, the organization will not reap the fruits of community learning. Next to knowledge-sharing as a routine and careful management, another key ingredient of the second wave of knowledge management could well be supporting the process of objectification.

2.4   Objectifying local knowledge

Objectification as an important aspect of learning refers to the process through which shared knowledge becomes accepted by the collective as being reliable, valuable and useful to use when acting as a participant of the organization. So far we have not given a great deal of explicit attention to this complex process. Instead, we have simply referred to it while discussing the various processes of knowledge-sharing separately.

Knowledge-sharing alone does not necessarily result in the (re)construction and development of organizational knowledge. Thus, next to providing stimuli to share knowledge as a routine, another aspect of the second wave in knowledge management is to build a bridge between individual learning and organizational learning. Von Krogh et al (2000) refer in this context to 'globalizing local knowledge'. Botkin (1999, p. 106) talks in this context about the need for a 'networked management' to integrate local knowledge within the organization as a whole. In his words:

> "A manager's chief role and practice is integration. The main goal is to create new knowledge by converting individual learning to organizational knowledge".

Supporting the process of objectification is needed in order for the organization as a whole to benefit from local knowledge-sharing practices. As mentioned earlier, many knowledge management initiatives do not include ways to transfer the results of individual learning processes to organizational knowledge. One of the consequences of focussing too much on individual learning, is that knowledge management will only flourish during periods of economic growth. Conversely, because they do not contribute to the organization as a whole, when an economic slump sets in this type of knowledge management initiative will be the first to be cut back.

As mentioned earlier, when describing the case of the NN claim processors and the consultants at Cap Gemini, a lot of learning takes place without organizations paying any attention to it. A lack of objectification is the cause of this incomplete learning (Huysman 1996), and March and Olsen (1976) refer to these incomplete organizational learning processes as manifestations of 'audience learning', while Kim (1993) talks about 'fragmented learning'. Audience learning or fragmented learning refers to situations in which individuals in the organization learn but the organization as a whole does not.

There are various ways to support the process of objectification so that knowledge shared by individuals becomes accepted by the organization as a whole. Objectification can take place via the intervention of 'domain experts', people who are considered to be the *primus interparus* (P.I.) among the community members. Most communities informally select one individual or a group of people to be the P.I. of the community. This person plays an important role in objectifying the knowledge that is shared between the communities. His or her acknowledgement of the knowledge as being relevant, innovative, useful etc. to the community will stimulate other members to use it. This corresponds with the idea of reference groups and significant others, concepts that were introduced a century ago by symbolic interactionists (Shibutani 1955, Thomas 1914). It is important that managers recognize these key people and take their knowledge seriously. If not, knowledge will be objectified but will only remain relevant to the community itself. As the case of Stork and Unilever illustrated, key community members also need to have a stake outside their community to support the acceptance of the value and usability of the knowledge by other organizational participants. Thus, in order for community knowledge to cross boundaries and become accepted by a larger audience, knowledge brokers are needed who are perceived as being the 'significant others'.

Next to a more natural role of senior members or experts, experts can also be used in a jury of people who peer-review the knowledge of their community members. We already discussed this way of objectification at IBM. In the following box an example is given of peer reviews as a way of objectifying community knowledge.

> **Eureka, a successful knowledge-sharing system (taken from Brown 2000, p. 17)**
> At Xerox, a Web-based system called 'Eureka' is used by photocopier repairmen ('reps') as a new way of accelerating their learning and structuring the community knowledge on how to act as a successful repairman. The problem with creating such a system was that many, if not all, of the reps knew that most of the ideas and stories about repairing copier machines that were floating around were not very reliable, they were merely opinions, and sometimes even fantastic horror stories. "To transform their opinions and experiences into 'warranted beliefs', hence actionable, contributors had to submit their

ideas for peer review, a process facilitated by the Web. The peers would quickly vet and refine the story, and connect it to others. In addition, the author attaches his or her name to the resulting story or tip, thus creating both intellectual and social capital, the latter because tech reps who create really great stories become local heroes and hence more central members of their community of practice."

Objectification might also be supported by top management through their explicit acknowledgement of the importance of communities of practice. This is the case at Unilever, but others have described similar examples (e.g. Botkin 1999, Brown and Duguid 1991, 2000, Cohen and Prusak 2000). Recognizing the importance of communities and networks requires an awareness of where valuable communities are located and what holds them together. This also involves the principles of 'hospitality' (Ciborra 1996) and that of 'doing no harm' (Cohen and Prusak 2000). The latter authors provide the following counter example of harming communities just by being ignorant of their existence and value to the company.

> **Harming communities through ignorance** (taken from Cohen and Prusak, 2000, pp. 77-78).
> "Through most of the 1980s, Chrysler was organized into functional departments: emissions systems, body, steering, electrical systems, and so forth. One group after another participated in the design of a new car, passing on its work to the next in line. At the end of the decade, the company began to reorganize around car 'platforms', or model types, instead of functions; those new groups included engineers in all the areas needed to produce a new car design. By most measures, the reorganization succeeded brilliantly, reducing design time by 25 percent and developing cars with more customer appeal than older models. Disturbingly, though, defects began cropping up in the new designs, many of them problems that had been successfully solved in the past. The company seemed to be forgetting some of what it knew about designing cars. Damage to components of social capital turned out to be the source of this organizational amnesia. The disbanded functional departments had been rich communities of relationships through which experienced engineers shared what they knew and trained and mentored newcomers. Successful in most ways, the reorganization that broke those departments into smaller groups disrupted important communities of practice, and problems resulted. The company did not know the communities were there, performing essential knowledge-sharing, until they disappeared".

2.5   New role of ICT

Investing in social capital seems even more important with the growth of virtual organizations and the continuous changes that are a result of shifting partnerships and boundaries. Due to these organizational changes, existing social capital can easily be shaken up. One way to help people connect despite geographic and time differences, is through the use of communication technology, such as e-mail, telephone, video-conferencing and more advanced GroupWare technologies.

It has already been argued for many years that GroupWare will be a very important tool in present and future organizational settings. However, so far, empirical studies that suggest the institutionalization of these tools in the group processes have been remarkably limited (e.g. Bowers 1994, Ciborra 1996, Orlikowski 1996, Zuboff 1988). There could be many explanations for this, but given what our cases tell us, perhaps the most convincing one is that people do not use these sophisticated tools simply because their need to share knowledge is limited. We believe that the use of GroupWare tools will start to increase the moment the value lies more in the network than in individuals.

The role of ICT in social capital can be seen as bi-directional. A high level of social capital, shown for example by pre-existing, strong non-electronic networks, is a success factor in establishing electronic-based networks (Fukuyama 1995). This is also what we saw happening in the cases discussed in this book. But at the same time, the existence of ICT possibilities might create a networking infrastructure, which encourages the formation of social capital (Calabrese and Borchert 1996). It is thus an empirical question which tendency will dominate.

The cases in this book, and also in others (e.g. Ciborra 1996, Davenport and Prusak 1998) illustrate that one of the most problematic aspects of knowledge management systems is when they require extra effort. In this way organizations are faced with the challenge of making the tool part of the work. This does not necessarily mean that the technology needs to adjust to the work. It is often not the technology that hinders knowledge-sharing, it is the culture. ICT is very helpful in supporting knowledge-sharing, but it should match the culture including its social capital. If people do not like to share knowledge, ICT tools will not change their minds. And the opposite is also true, if people want to share knowledge, they will use whatever is at hand to support it. In this respect, Levi-Strauss' concept of bricolage is very relevant, namely the ability to 'make do with 'whatever is to hand' (1966, p. 17).

Nowadays, systems built to exchange knowledge such as repository systems are often well designed without technical failures. It is wrong to blame the technology; it is the belief in technology as opposed to people that should be blamed. Systems do not make collaboration happen. Cohen and Saidel (2000) argue that a predisposition of people to help each other and using the system as part of daily work practices are the two most important conditions that make collaboration happen. It is only when these conditions are met, that people will make use of ICT knowledge management systems (see also Box "Social capital and the success of RRAccess"). The case story described by Saidel and Cohen (2000) tells how a group of people at Russell Reynolds Associates actively used the knowledge base both to acquire and to store knowledge. The 'high social capital' of the organization created a feeling of mutuality, trust and collective involvement, which prompted the participants to use the system routinely.

Social capital and the success of RRAccess (Taken from Saidel and Cohen (2000)

Russell Reynolds Associates is a large executive search firm with 35 offices in 18 countries ranging in size from three employees to 90. At the firm, the recruiters' task is to find the best possible candidate for their clients all over the world. The executive search business is very competitive and relies heavily on networks of relationships. At this high level, information about possible candidates as well as about the profile cannot be exchanged without an in-depth account of expectations, reputations and experience. Certainly in this business, knowledge of who the right people are and where to find them is power. Although recruiters with the largest network are the best in the business, the search for the best candidate usually lies beyond the capability of one recruiter. Because of the global scale of the business, the success of recruiting largely depends on one's ability to collaborate and share knowledge with others. To support this collaboration, recruiters at RRA meet every week to learn about their colleagues' assignments and to offer help. Because of this professional need to share knowledge with each other, mutual help is not just restricted to the formal Monday morning meetings.

According to Saidel and Cohen, recruiters constantly inform each other and share their networks. These social network ties are further built on a foundation of mutual trust and transparency and a supportive reward system. Because trust relies heavily on knowing 'what is going on', colleagues know what others are doing and what they are up against. Also, members of RRA are evaluated on their collaboration by thorough evaluation processes in which mentors, supervisors, subordinates and peers judge whether a member freely offers information to colleagues and works well as a team member. With more than 750 members and its geographic dispersion, it is impossible for anyone to know everyone, or know everything about the assignments. Like most growing companies, RRA uses technology to keep firm members connected and to capture and preserve its collective memory. The global proprietary database, RRAccess, contains records of every assignment along with relevant and detailed information on all of the candidates the firm has considered for each assignment.

In contrast to most repository systems, RRA recruiters all over the world use the system in the course of their daily work. The system carries out the search process and makes its results transparent for everyone. According to the writers, trust and mutual engagement makes it possible and desirable for members to 'know each other's business'. This sense of mutuality also contributes to the quality of material in the system. RRAccess is not meant to contain all the knowledge of the firm or replace direct contact between colleagues. By allowing recruiters to see the details of search activity in the firm and identifying those individuals who have the experience that could be relevant to their current work, it helps them find the right people to talk to.

At the time the case story was written, the system had been in use for two years. This is not long enough to be certain about its success. However, the story provides an illustration of a system that is used extensively because it reflects the culture and enhances the daily work routines of the people working at the firm.

It is important to stress again that by our critical perspective on ICT and knowledge management, we do not wish to reject the use of databases to support knowledge management. As organizational practices such as the ones discussed in chapter 4 illustrate, codifying past experiences might indeed be highly useful and relevant. Knowledge bases find almost universal acceptance, even in cultures alien to sharing knowledge. This is because they do something each individual needs to do – stay up to date on information critical to performing one's job (Botkin 1999). But the issue is how to ensure a high level of quality of the knowledge stored in the knowledge base. We believe that investing in social capital will stimulate the need to contribute to the collective knowledge space.

3. RECOMMENDATIONS FOR MANAGING KNOWLEDGE-SHARING

As a way of ending the book, we have used this last section to summarize the various recommendations made throughout this book to support managing knowledge-sharing in the second generation.

Increase individual involvement and the involvement of the organization as a whole
Routine knowledge-sharing takes place specifically in organizations where there is individual involvement and trust. Inquisitiveness, learning from one another and keeping abreast of new developments are the driving force behind knowledge-sharing. The same applies whenever there is considerable involvement in the goal or mission of an organization; the collective desire to contribute to a higher goal often stimulates mutual knowledge exchange. Although it is hard to get these different situations of interpersonal and organizational involvement off the ground, such ideal-typical situations can serve as role models from which reflective questions can be derived, such as: Do people get the chance to feel that they are involved with each other? Could the gulf between the individual and the organization be too great to create involvement? Do local social structures such as communities and informal networks provide an alternative to improve mutual participation? Is the organization's mission inspiring enough for the employees to feel personally involved?

Exercise caution about rewarding knowledge-sharing
The idea that knowledge-sharing ought to be rewarded originates from the idea that knowledge-sharing requires extra effort. When knowledge-sharing becomes routine there is no question of extra effort taking place and a reward in itself can actually prove counterproductive. Dishing out financial incentives only has an impact in the short-term. The reward in this case represents compensation for some effort that would not otherwise materialize in the absence of this incentive. A more tacit reward system has more of an impact in the long term than a financial one. A tacit reward can be to allow someone's input into knowledge-sharing weigh in their favour during employee appraisal interviews.

Encourage a knowledge-friendly culture
Knowledge management thrives best of all in a stimulating culture, but such a culture cannot be imposed from above. Culture evolves over a long period through the way in which individuals work with one another. Several methods can be used to influence the culture, among which the most important are those that adapt the selection criteria and the standards used to evaluate performance. A positive evaluation of someone's knowledge-friendly attitude will eventually be effective. Similarly, creating opportunities for growth and working in a variety of different teams, ensures that people eventually both get to know each other and learn from one another.

Avoid the feeling that knowledge-sharing is an extra chore
As long as the feeling that knowledge-sharing is an extra chore prevails, it will never become part of the day-to-day operations. Management can get around this by making knowledge-sharing engaging and necessary rather than tedious and enforced. Adding content to the intranet, for example, is often seen as being too much like hard work while participating in personal networks, communities and informal gatherings is more likely to be perceived as being enjoyable, even though intranet use actually requires less time than it takes to participate in personal networks. Even so, the pressures of time can weigh so heavily in the case of personal contacts that people would rather wriggle out of them. Moreover, managers increasing the time that employees can spend on knowledge-sharing is no longer an option in present day labour relations. Professional staff often have their own personal set of objectives and deadlines. What is important in the end, is that the work is organized so that employees experience knowledge-sharing as an integral part of it. A first step towards doing this is to perceive learning as inextricably bound up with working and to approach organizations as if they were 'communities of communities' (Brown and Duguid 1991) rather than hierarchies.

Actively involve managers in knowledge-sharing
Organization-wide participation in knowledge-sharing requires an active contribution from those in managerial positions rather than having them merely direct the process. Their input is crucial if an organization is striving towards

knowledge-sharing as a way of thinking and operating. Managers have a primary responsibility in ensuring that staff share their knowledge with each other, that they are receptive to other people's knowledge, and that they actively participate in social networks. This type of stimulating culture can only be created through a hands-on approach. It is also important for managers to set an inspirational example.

Invest in social capital

Investing in social capital has serious implications for managers (Raider and Burt 1996). Managers should first of all understand the importance of social capital. Insight into the degree of organizational social capital can be measured by social network analysis. These analyses can be useful in understanding how, for example, the company really works in terms of communication structures, information flows, and what skills are really perceived as being valuable. It can also be used to anticipate catalysts and bottlenecks such as organizational changes, and to understand the importance of diversity, etc. Social network analysis can also be helpful as a selection mechanism. Selection criteria should then include recognition of people's active membership in various social networks. Of course, social network analysis alone cannot be used as a tool to manage people and organizations. The moment network structures are made explicit and visible, connections between people might already have changed. Also, it is still questionable whether these analyses are able to visualize the various dimensions (cognitive, structural and relational) of existing social networks.

Be wary of creating formal knowledge management positions

A typical feature of many knowledge-sharing initiatives is that they create separate positions, such as those of Corporate Knowledge Officer (CKO), knowledge coordinator, and knowledge manager. Whenever organizations strive to make knowledge-sharing routine, separately created positions tend to work counterproductively. First of all, there is always the danger of duplicating responsibilities. Is action preferred when based on a responsibility towards knowledge management or in the name of operational responsibility? In practice, it would seem that this confusion often results in the second option being selected. Another danger is that a 'Corporate Knowledge Officer' cannot oversee everything. Knowledge is omnipresent. It is therefore difficult, and maybe even impossible, to give somebody full responsibility for this. Furthermore, individuals are less inclined to take on the responsibility themselves when others have been designated as having full responsibility for it. This works counterproductively as everybody is responsible for knowledge-sharing.

Ensure that support from top management is forthcoming

Initiatives for structured knowledge-sharing flourish when they are supported by top management. Support from top management is necessary to relay the message that knowledge-sharing is critical for the organization. Support is needed to attract funding and create an infrastructure. Nevertheless, support from top management is not always a universal panacea. One of the dangers of interference from above is that the need for knowledge-sharing will then come from the top down. Top managers would therefore be better advised to limit their involvement to providing (financial) support and relaying the message. The way in which knowledge-sharing evolves in practice is up to the knowledge workers themselves, with the support of the line managers.

Be circumspect about measuring knowledge-sharing
If knowledge-sharing does actually contribute to the added value of an organization, then organizations tend to prefer to have this written down in black and white prior to investing in it. However, more and more organizations are beginning to realize that knowledge and knowledge-sharing are not subjects that lend themselves well to quantitative analysis. The danger of determining the financial benefits of knowledge-sharing lies in measuring it using the wrong standards: the number of hits via the Internet, the number of active and passive contributions to meetings and the number of written reports. The results of knowledge-sharing practices that may have an even greater impact on organizational operations, such as those taking place through informal conversations, communities and personal networks cannot be expressed in financial terms.

Support knowledge-sharing using a multidisciplinary approach
Managing knowledge-sharing requires active input from a variety of disciplines: together with the ICT manager and the human resources manager, members of top management and others who have direct managerial responsibility should play an active role here. It is not necessary for all these managers to initiate knowledge-sharing directly. A knowledge-sharing initiative is often sparked off from within the confines of a project or operational unit. In practice it would appear that this is especially suited to ICT-driven initiatives, such as implementing an intranet. If it is to succeed, it is important that different managers develop the initiative further and give it their full support.

Respect the organization's ICT past
It is important to be familiar with the knowledge and skills that are already present within the organization before introducing a new technology. If the staff have limited computer experience then this will not change simply by introducing an intranet. Many organizations make the mistake of not paying enough attention to their ICT history. As long as people perceive technology as being complex or irritating then this can only have a negative impact upon knowledge-sharing. Knowledge-sharing should not impose additional burdens upon staff. This is especially true whenever a lengthy or intensive training programme is required to use ICT. A step-by-step method is preferable to instantly implementing technology that requires staff training and a familiarity with the programme. Also ICT's role should be derived from the need for knowledge and knowledge-sharing instead of the other way round.

Focus on connecting people rather than capturing knowledge
Linking people up with one another is more important that capturing and disseminating knowledge. Or as Prusak puts it:

> "If you have a dollar to spend on knowledge management, it's better spent on connection than capture".

The possibility for personal interaction appears to be important among employees, also when knowledge-sharing is supported by ICT-based knowledge systems. In order to use the system, it is important to be knowledgeable about the identity of the person providing the knowledge, what are his or her positive and negative experiences with regard to using the knowledge and the extent to which the knowledge lends itself to reuse. For this purpose, personal contact with the knowledge transporter is crucial. Likewise, the existing personal network is also an important stimulus to contribute to the knowledge base. A culture that stimulates reciprocity as well as knowing who will benefit from the knowledge and for what purpose, will encourage people to add to the system. At all the organizations where we carried out research we saw this crop up again and again: personal contact wins hands down every time.

REFERENCES

Abrahamson, E. (1996), "Management fashion", *Academy of Management Review*, vol 21/1 pp 254-285.

Abercrombie, N., S. Hill and B.S. Turner (1984), Dictionary of Sociology, Penguin Books.

Aldrich, H. and D. Herker (1977), "Boundary spanning roles and organizational structure", *Academy of Management Review*, April, pp. 217-230.

Argyris, Ch. (1990), Overcoming organizational defenses: facilitating organizational learning, Needham Heights, MA: Allyn and Bacon.

Argyris Ch. and D. Schön (1978), Organizational learning a theory of action-perspective" Reading, MA: Addison-Wesley.

Becker, G. (1964), Human Capital, a theoretical and empirical analysis with special reference to education, New York: Columbia University.

Berger, P. and T. Luckman (1966), The social construction of knowledge, London: Penguin books.

Bertrams, J. (1999), De kennisdelende organisatie: kunst en praktijk van het hergebruik van kennis, Schiedam: Scriptum.

Blackler, F. (1995), "Knowledge, knowledge work and organizations: an overview and interpretation", *Organization Studies*, vol 16/6 pp. 1021-1046.

Boisot, M. (1998), Knowledge Assets: Securing Competitive Advantage in the Information Economy, Oxford University Press.

Boland, R.J. and R.V. Tenkasi, R.V. (1995), "Perspective making and perspective taking in communities of knowing", *Organization Science*, 6(4), pp. 350-372.

Bontis, N. (1999), "Managing Organizational Knowledge by Diagnosing Intellectual Capital: Framing and Advancing the State of the Field", *International Journal of Technology Management*.

Botkin, J. (1999), Smart Business: how knowledge communities can revolutionize your company, New York: Free Press.

Bowers, J. (1994), "The work to make a network work: studying CSCW in action". *Proceedings of CSCW'94*, Chapel Hill, NC: ACM Press.

Brown, J.S. (2000), "Growing up Digital, the web and the new learning ecology", *Change, the magazine of higher learning*, March/April, pp. 11-22

Brown, J.S. and P. Duguid (1991), "Organizational learning and communities of practice: towards a unified view of working, learning and innovation", *Organization Science*, 2/1.

Brown, J.S. and P. Duguid (2000a), "Practice vs. Process: the tension that won't go away", *Knowledge Directions*, vol 2/1, pp. 86- 96.

Brown, J.S. and P. Duguid (2000b), The Social Life of Information, Harvard Business School Press, Cambridge MA.

Burt, R.S. (1992), Structural holes: the social structure of competition, Harvard University Press, Cambridge.

Calabrese, A. And M. Borchert (1996), "Prospects for electronic democracy in the United States: Rethinking communications and social policy", *Media, Culture, and Society* 18: 249-268.

Ciborra, C.U. and G.F. Lanzara (1994), "Formative contexts and information technology, understanding the dynamics of innovation in organizations", *Accounting, Management and Information Technology*, vol. 4/2.

Ciborra, C.U. (ed.) (1996), Groupware and Teamwork, John Wiley and Sons.

Cicourel, A.V. (1973), Cognitive Sociology: Language and Meaning in Social Interaction, New York: Penguin Press.

Choo, C.W. (1998), The Knowing organization: how organizations use information to construct meaning, create knowledge and make decisions, New York: Oxford University Press.

Choo, C.W., B. Detlor and D. Turnbull (2000), WebWork, information seeking and knowledge work on the world wide web, Kluwer Academic Publishers.

Cohen, M.D. and D. Levinthal (1990), "Absoptive Capacity: a new perspective on learning and innovation", *Administrative Science Quarterly*, March, pp. 128-152.

Coleman, J.S. (1988), "Social Capital in the Creation of Human Capital", *American Journal of Sociology* (Supplement) 94 (1988), pp. 95-120,

Coleman, J.S. (1990), The Foundations of Social Theory, Cambridge: Harvard University Press.

Cook, S.D.N. and D.Yanow. (1993), "Culture and Organizational Learning", *Journal of Management Inquiry*, 2/4.

Cyert, R.M and J.G. March. (1963), A behavioral theory of the firm, Englewood Cliffs, Prentice Hall.

Davenport, T.H. (1997), "Ten Principles of Knowledge Management and Four Case Studies", *Knowledge and Process Management*, vol 4/3.

Davenport, T.H. and L. Prusak (1998), Working Knowledge: how organizations manage what they know, Boston: Harvard Business School Press.

Davenport, T. H., D. W. de Long, and M. C. Beers (1998), "Successful knowledge management projects", *Sloan Management Review*, 30, pp. 43-57.

Davenport, T.H. and P. Klahr (1998), "Managing customer support knowledge", *California Management Review*, 40 (3), pp. 195-208.

Den Hertog, F and E. Huizinga (1997), De Kennisfactor, concurreren als kennisonderneming, Deventer.

DiMaggio, P.J. and W.W. Powell (1983), "The iron cage revisited: Institutional isomorphism and collective rationality in organizational fields", *American Sociological Review*, vol 48, pp. 147-160.

Dixon, N.M. (2000), Common Knowledge, Cambridge MA: Harvard Business School Press

Dodgson, M. (1993a), "Learning, trust and technological collaboration", *Human Relations*, vol 46, pp. 77-95.

Dodgson, M. (1993b), "Organizational Learning: A Review of Some Literatures", *Organization Studies*, vol 14/3, pp. 375-394.

Douglas, M. (1987), How Institutions Think, London: Routledge & Kegan Paul.

Drew, S. (1999), Building Knowledge Management into Strategy: Making Sense of a New Perspective, *Long Range Planning*, vol 32, no. 1, pp 130-136.

Drucker, P. (1993), Post-capitalist Society. Oxford: Butterworth-Heinemann.

Duffy Daintry, (1998), "Knowledge champions", *CIO Enterprise Management*, Nov.15.

Durkheim, E. (1978), On institutional analysis, Chicago: Chicago University Press.

Earl Michael J., Ian A. Scott (1999), "What is a chief knowledge officer", *Sloan Management Review*, winter, vol 40, 2, pp. 29-38.

Easterby-Smith, M., L. Araujo and J. Burgoyne (eds.) (1999), Organizational Learning and the Learning Organization: Developments in Theory and Practice, Sage.

Edvinsson, L. and M.S. Malone. (1997) Intellectual Capital: realizing your company's true value by finding its hidden roots. New York: Harper Business,

Elkjaer, B. (1999) "Organizational learning: A management tool or part of human interaction?" In: Easterby-Smith, M., L. Araujo and J. Burgoyne (eds.), *Organizational Learning and the Learning Organization: Developments in Theory and Practice*, Sage.

Fahey, L. and L. Prusak (1998), "The eleven deadliest sins of knowledge management", *California Management Review*, 40 (3), 265-276.

Fountain, J.E. (1997), "Social Capital: a key enabler of innovation in science and technology", In: Branscomb and Keller (eds) *Investing in Innovation: Toward a consensus strategy for federal technology policy*, Cambridge: MIT Press.

Fukuyama, F. (1995), Trust: the social virtues and the creation of prosperity, New York: Free Press.

Gambetta, D. (1988), Trust: Making and breaking cooperative relations, Blackwell: New York.

Garvin, D.A. (1993), "Building a learning organization", *Harvard Business Review*, vol 71/4, pp. 78-91.

Gergen, K.J (1994), Realities and Relationships, soundings in social construction, Cambridge MA, Harvard University Press.

Geus, De, A.P. (1988), "Planning as learning", *Harvard Business Review*, March-April.

Gherardi, S., D. Nicolini, and F. Odella (1998), "Towards a social understanding of how people learn in organizations", *Management Learning*, vol 29 (3), pp. 273-297.

Gherardi, S. (2000), "Practice-based theorizing on learning and knowing in organizations", *Organization Studies*, vol 7 (2), pp. 211-223.

Giddens, A. (1984), The constitution of society, Polity Press, Cambridge.

Glazer, R. (1998), "Measuring the Knower: towards a theory of knowledge equity", *California Management Review*, pp. 175-194.

Gottschalk, P (1999), "Use of IT for knowledge management in law firms", *Journal of Information, Law and Technology*, 3.

Granovetter, M (1985),"Economic Action and Social Structure: The Problem of Embeddedness," *American Journal of Sociology* 91 pp. 481-510.

Grant, RM (1996), "Toward a knowledge-based theory of the firm", *Strategic Management Journal*, 17 (Winter), pp. 109-122.

Grieken van, H. (1999), "Kijk maar op CapCom", *Management & Informatie*, vol 4, 49-58.

Hakansson, H. and J. Johanson (eds), Business Network Learning, Oxford: Elsevier Science Publications, pp. 17-32.

Hansen M. T., B. von Oetinger (2001), "Introducing T-shaped managers, knowledge management's next generation", *Harvard Business Review*, March, pp 107-116.

Hansen M.T, N. Nohria and T. Tierney (1999), "What's your strategy for managing knowledge?", *Harvard Business Review*, March-April, pp. 108-116.

Hanson, M.T. (1999), "The Search-Transfer Problem: the role of weak ties in sharing knowledge across organization sub-units", *Administrative Science Quarterly*, pp. 82-111.

Hargadon, A.B. (1998), "Firms as Knowledge Brokers: Lessons in Pursuing Continuous Innovation", *California Management Review*. 40 (3): pp. 209-227.

Hertog, F. den and E. Huizinga (1997), De kennisfactor. Concurreren als kennisonderneming. Deventer.

Holtham, C. and V. Ward (2000), "Physical Space – the most neglected resource in contemporary knowledge management", *Proceedings of the Knowledge Management Conference*, Birmingham UK.

Hosking, D.M. and I.E. Morley (1991), A social psychology of organizing, New York: Harvester Wheatsheaf.

Huber, G.P (1991), "Organizational learning: the contributing processes and the literatures", *Organizational Science*, vol 2/1, pp. 88-115.

Huysman, M.H. (1996), Dynamics of organizational learning. Amsterdam: Thesis Publishers.

Huysman, M.H. (2000a), "Organizational Learning or Learning Organizations", *European Journal of Work and Organizational Psychology*, vol 9/2, pp. 133-145.

182

Huysman, M.H. (2000b), "Rethinking Organizational Learning", Accountancy, *Management and Information Technology*, vol 10.

Huysman, M.H and P. van Baalen (2002), "Knowledge Management, Communities and Social Capital", *Trends in Communication*, vol 8.

Jacobs, D. (1999), Het kennisoffensief: Slim concurreren in de kenniseconomie. Deventer: Samson.

Jordan, B. (1989), "Cosmopolitical obstetrics: some insights from the training of traditional midwives", *Social Science and Medicine*, 28/9.

Kanter, R.M. (1990), When giants learn to dance: the challenge of strategy, management and careers in the 1990's, London: Simon and Shuster.

Kim, D.H. (1993), "The link between individual and organizational learning", *Sloan Management Review*, Fall, pp. 37-50.

Kessels, J. (2000), Verleiden tot Kennisproductiviteit, Universiteit Twente.

Kieser, A. (1997), "Rhetoric and myth in management fashion", *Organization*, vol 4. pp 49-74.

Krackhardt, D. (1992), "The strength of strong ties: The importance of philos", in N. Nohria and R. Eccles (Eds.), *Networks and Organizations: Structure, Form, and Action*, pp. 216-239. Boston: Harvard Business School Press

Lave, J. and E.Wenger (1991), Situated Learning: Legitimate Peripheral Participation, Cambridge: Cambridge University Press.

Leonard, D. (1995), Wellsprings of knowledge: building and sustaining the sources of innovation. Boston: Harvard Business School Press.

Leonard, D. and S. Sensiper (1998), "The role of tacit knowledge in group innovation", *California Management Review*, vol 40/3, pp. 112-132.

Leonard, D. and W. Swap (2000), "Gurus in the Garage", *Harvard Business Review*, Nov.-Dec., pp. 71-82.

Lesser, E.L. (ed) (2000), Knowledge and Social Capital; foundations and applications. Boston: Butterworth Heinemann.

Levis-Strauss, C. (1966), The Savage Mind. Chicago: University of Chicago Press.

Levitt, B. and J.G. March (1988), "Organizational Learning", *Annual Review Sociology*, vol 14, pp. 319-340.

Loury, G.C. (1987), "Why Should We Care About Group Inequality?" *Social Philosophy and Policy* 5 pp. 249-71.

Malhotra, Y. (2000), "From Information Management to Knowledge Management: Beyond the 'Hi-Tech Hidebound' Systems". In: K. Srikantaiah and M.E.D. Koenig (eds.), *Knowledge Management for the Information Professional*. Medford, N.J.: Information Today Inc., pp 37-61.

Malone, Th. W. and R. J. Laubacher (1998), "The dawn of the e-lance economy", *Harvard Business Review*, Sep/Oct , pp. 144-152.

March, J.G. (1988), Decisions and Organizations, Oxford: Basil Blackwell.

March, J.G. and H.A. Simon (1993), Organizations, second edition, Cambridge MA: Blackwell Publishers.

Markus, M.(1991), "Toward a 'critical mass' theory of interactive media", In: J. Fulk and C. Steinfield (eds.), *Organizations and communication technology* (pp. 194-218). Newbury Park, CA: Sage

March J.G. (1991), "Exploration and exploitation in organizational learning", *Organizational Science*, vol 2/1, pp. 71-87.

March, J.G. and J.P. Olsen (1976), Ambiguity and choice in organizations, Bergen, Norway: Universitetsforlaget.

Marquardt, M.J. (1996), Building the Learning Organization. New York: McGraw-Hill.

McDermott, R. (1998), "Why information technology inspired but cannot deliver knowledge management". *California Management Review* 41 (4), pp. 103-117.

Miles, R.H. and W.A. Randolf (1980), "Influence of organizational learning styles on early development", In: J.R. Kimberly and R.H. Miles (eds) *The organizational life cycle: issues in the creation, transformation, and decline of organizations*, San Francisco: Jossey-Bass, pp. 44-82.

Moorman, C. and A.S. Miner (1998), "Organizational improvisation and organizational memory", *Academy of Management Review*, 23-4, pp. 698-724.

Morgan, G. (1986), Images of Organization, Newsbury Park, CA: Sage Publications.

Morgan, G. and R. Ramirez (1983), "Action learning: a holographic metaphor for guiding social change", *Human Relations*, vol 7/1, pp. 1-28.

Nahapiet, J. and S. Ghoshal (1998), "Social capital, intellectual capital, and the organizational advantage". *Academy of Management Review*, vol. 23, no. 2, pp. 242-266

Nelson, R. and S.G. Winter (1982), An evolutionary theory of economic change, Cambridge, MA: Addison-Wesley.

Nicolini, D. and M.B. Meznar (1995), "The Social Construction of Organizational Learning: Conceptual and Practical Issues in the Field", *Human Relations*, vol. 48, No. 7, pp. 727-746

Nonaka, I. and H.Takeuchi (1995), The knowledge creating company. New York: Oxford University Press.

Orlikowski, W. (1996), "Evolving with Notes, Organizational change around groupware technology". In: C.U Ciborra (ed.) *Groupware and Teamwork*, John Wiley and Sons.

Orr, J.E. (1990), "Sharing knowledge, celebrating identity: community memory in a service culture". In: P. Middleton and D. Edwards (eds.) *Collective remembering: memory in society*, London: Sage.

Parsons, T. (1960), Structure and process in modern societies, Glencoe: The Free Press.

Pedler, M., J. Burgoyne, and T. Boydell (1991), The learning company, McGraw Hill Book Company.

Pentland, B.T. (1995), "Information systems and organizational learning: The social epistemology of organizational knowledge systems", *Accounting, Management and Information Technology*, vol 5, pp. 1-21.

Polanyi, M. (1958), The tacit dimension, New York: Anchor.

Porter, M.E. (1980), Competitive strategy: Techniques for analyzing industries and competitors, New York: The Free Press.

Porter, M.E (1990), The competitive advantage of nations, London: MacMillan.

Powell, W.W. and P.J. DiMaggio (eds) (1991), The new institutionalism in organizational analysis, Chicago: University of Chicago Press

Powell, W.W., K.W. Koput and L. Smith-Doerr (1996), "Interorganizational collaboration and the locus of innovation: networks of learning in biotechnology", *Administrative Science Quarterly*, vol 41/1, pp. 116-145.

Prahalad, C.K. and G. Hamel (1990), "The core competence of the corporation", *Harvard Business Review*, May-June, pp. 79-91.

Putnam, R.D. (1993), "The Prosperous Community: Social Capital and Public Life", *American Prospect* 13, pp. 35-42

Putnam, R.D., (2000), Bowling Alone. The collapse and revival of American community, New York: Simon & Schuster .

Raider, H.J. and R.S. Burt (1996), The Boundaryless Career: A New Employment Principle for a new Organizational Era, Oxford: Oxford University Press.

Roos, J., Roos, G., Dragonetti, N. and L. Edvinsson (1998). Intellectual Capital: Navigating in the New Business Landscape, New York: New York University Press.

Rosenberg, N. and C. Frischtak (eds) (1985), International technological transfer, New York: Praeger.

Saidel, B. and D. Cohen (2000), "Russel Reynolds Associates, The power of Social Capital", *Knowledge Connections*, Spring, pp. 6 –21.

Sandelands, L.E. and R.E. Stablein. (1987), "The concept of organization mind", In: S. Bacharach and N. DiTomaso (eds.) *Research in the sociology of organizations,* vol 5, Greenwich, CT: JAI Press, pp. 135-161.

Sandelands, L.E. and R. Drazin (1989), On the language of organization theory*, Organization Studies*, vol 10, pp. 457-478.

Sandelands, L.E. and V. Srivatsan (1993), "The problem of experience in the study of organizations", *Organization Studies*, pp. 1-22.

Scarbrough, H. and J. Swan (2001), "Explaining the diffusion of knowledge management: the role of fashion", *British Journal of Management*, vol 12, pp. 3-12.

Schein, E.H. (1992), Organizational culture and leadership 2nd edition, San Fransisco: Jossey-Bass.

Schumpeter, J. (1934), The theory of economic development, Cambridge: Harvard University Press.

Schutz, A. (1971), Collected Papers, vol 1 and 2, The Hague: Nijhoff

Scott, W.R. (1987), "The adolescene of institutional theory", *Administrative Science Quarterly* vol 32, pp. 493-511.

Senge, P. (1992), The fifth discipline, the art & practice of the learning organization, Randon House London.

Shibutani, T. (1955), "Reference groups as perspectives", *American Journal of Sociology*, vol 60, pp. 562-569.

Sims, D. (1999), "Organizational Learning as the Development of Stories", In: Easterby-Smith, M., L. Araujo and J. Burgoyne (eds.), *Organizational Learning and the Learning Organization: Developments in Theory and Practice*, Sage.

Spender, J.C. (1996), "Making knowledge the basis of a dynamic strategy of the firm", *Strategic Management Journal*, 17, pp. 45-62

Star, S.L. (1992), "The trojan door: organizations, work and the 'open black box'", *Systems Practice*, vol 5.

Stein, E.W (1995) "Organizational memory: Review of concepts and recommendations for management", *International Journal of Information Management*, vol 15/2, pp. 17-32.

Stein, E.W. and V. Zwass (1995), "Actualizing organizational memory with information systems" *Information Systems Research*, vol 6/2, pp. 85-117.

Stewart, T.A. (1997), Intellectual Capital: the new wealth of organizations, New York: Doubleday.

Sveiby, K.E. (1997), The New Organizational Wealth: Managing and Measuring Knowledge Based Assets. London: Berrett-Koehler.

Swan, J., J. Scarbrough, and J. Preston (1998), "Knowledge management – the next fad to forget people? ", *Proceedings of the 7th European Conference on Information Systems, Copenhagen Business School*, Denmark, pp. 668-678.

Szulanski, G. (1996), "Exploring internal stickiness: impediments to the transfer of best practice within the firm", *Strategic Management Journal*, vol 17, pp. 27-43.

Teece, D. (1998), "Capturing value from knowledge assets" *California Management Review*, 40(3), pp. 55-79

Thatchenkery, T.J. (1996), "Organizational learning, language games and knowledge creation", Editorial note, *Journal of Organizational Change Management*, vol 9/1, pp. 4-11.

Thomas, W.I. (1914),"The Prussian-Polish Situation: An Experiment in Assimilation", *American Journal of Sociology*, 19, pp. 624-639.

Tsang, E. (1997), "Organizational learning and the learning organization: A dichotomy between descriptive and prescriptive research", *Human Relations*, 50 (1), pp. 73-90.

Von Krogh, C. (1998), "Care in knowledge creation", *California Management Review* 40 (3), pp. 133-153.

Von Krogh, G., K. Ichijo, and I. Nonaka (2000), Enabling knowledge creation, Oxford University Press.

Walsh, J.P. and G.R. Ungson. (1991), "Organizational memory" *Academy of Management Review*, vol 16/1, pp. 57-91.

Weggeman, M. (1997), Kennismanagement, Schiedam: Scriptum

Weggeman M. (2000), Kennismanagement: de praktijk, Schiedam, Scriptum.

Weick, K.E. (1979), The Social Psychology of Organizing, Reading, MA: Addison-Wesley.

Weick, K.E. and K.H. Roberts (1993), "Collective mind in organizations: heedful inerrelating on flight desks", *Administrative Science Quarterly*, vol 38/3, pp. 357-381.

Weick, K.E. and F. Westley (1996), "Organizational learning: Affirming an oxymoron", In S. R. Clegg, C. Hardy and W. R. Nord (Eds.), *Handbook of Organization Studies*. Thousand Oaks, CA: Sage Publications, pp. 440- 458.

Wenger, E. (1998), Communities of practice, New York Cambridge University Press.

Wiigg, K.M. (1999), "What future knowledge management users may expect", *Journal of Knowledge Management*, vol 3/2 pp. 155-165.

Yanow, D. (2000), "Seeing organizational learning: a cultural view", *Organization*, 7/2, pp. 247-268.

Zack, M.H (1999), "Managing codified knowledge", *Sloan Management Review*, vol. 40, No. 4, Summer, pp. 45-58.

Zuboff, S. (1988), In the age of the smart machine, New York: Basic Books.

INDEX

ENDNOTES

[1] Organizations might also have different motives for supporting knowledge-sharing. With regard to this, knowledge-sharing is often supported for the benefit of solving problems. Meetings, conferences, and discussions all share a common feature and that is to support knowledge-sharing in order to solve problems. In this book, we do not take these forms of 'decision making' into account as motives for sharing knowledge. Rather, we limit ourselves to knowledge-sharing for the benefit of learning processes by and within organizations.

[2] This discussion is partly based on earlier publications (Huysman 1996, Huysman 2000).

[3] It should be noted that we do not use a pure process definition since we use 'achievement verbs' instead of process verbs (Sandelands and Drazin 1989). However, according to Weick and Westly (1996), 'organizational learning' is a concept that refers both to a process as well as to an outcome of that process and thus needs to be treated as such.

[4] The 'moments' of Berger and Luckman correspond to a certain extent to Giddens' structuration theory (1984). Giddens is one of the most well-known contemporary sociologists who proposes a dialectical relationship between action and structure. Action and structure pre-suppose each other, instead of being mutually exclusive. Giddens is more explicit than Berger and Luckman (1966) about the possible occurrence of the consequences of human action that are unknown or unintended.

[5] The latter is due to a restrictive policy adopted by the Railways to keep ticket sales on the train to an absolute minimum.

[6] The way in which we value these employees' contribution to the knowledge process is strikingly different in Western society compared to Japan. Japan, with its stress on continuous improvement and innovation, places a strong emphasis on the input of production workers to the knowledge building process and the improvement of key processes (Nonaka and Takeuchi 1994). Clear feedback is hereby given from the production worker's point of view via the team to the main process. Based on experiences with Total Quality Management, a Japanese worker's contribution is afforded an important place in the quality improvement process, in stark contrast to the more procedural interpretation in Western countries. Based on this tradition, Japanese companies place a high value on the tacit dimension of knowledge. In Western countries great value is placed on tacit knowledge in particular that can be turned into explicit knowledge.

[7] Unilever Research provides perhaps one of the most frequently quoted practical examples of how to facilitate a community (see eg. Von Krogh, 1998).

[8] Taken from a report, entitled "Connecting Intelligence", Ministry of Housing, Spatial Planning and the Environment, 1999

[9] idem

[10] Based on the report 'Connecting Intelligence 1999, interviews with four project leaders, and with the research institute responsible for the evaluation of the various projects.

[11] See among others, the books of Nonaka & Takeuchi (1995) and Weggeman (1996) and the 'best practices' cases of British Petroleum and Arthur Andersson.

[12] It should be noted that in cases of financial crises, knowledge management initiatives are often the first to be cut by management. This happened for example with the knowledge-sharing initiative at ING Barings.

[13] IBM report on knowledge-sharing

[14] Malone and Laubacher (1998) describe the e-lance economy as a world where the traditional hierarchical corporation has been replaced by a new organizational order of networked small organizations.

[15] See for example books like Boisot (1998), Brown and Duguid (2000), Cohen and Prusak (2001), Wenger, Snyder and McDermot (in press).